Higher Level Love

Growing Our Relationship Together

workbook 1

Higher Level Love

Growing Our Relationship Together

workbook 1

A Couples Program
Dr. Catherine Wheeler

workbook 1

Growing Our Relationship Together

Week 1	Opening Up our Relationship
Week 2	Moving out of "Blaming"
Week 3	Taking Down our "Walls"
Week 4	Increasing Emotional Trust
Week 5	Giving and Receiving Feedback
Week 6	Communication & "Feeling Heard"
Week7	Our "Baggage" is our Weakest Link
Week 8	Growing Together- Are we at risk?

LOVE'S PROMISE and POTENTIAL

When we start our relationships and families we are full of the hope, promise and wonder of new love. We have a vision that love will be rich, full, and nourishing. We have dreamed of this for years. Most of us believe if we find "the right person" it will be fulfilled. Unfortunately this isn't realistic and it's more of a fantasy than reality. We are more likely to create a relationship based on the patterns and programming we have inherited from our parents' personalities, from their relationship with us, and from their patterns. Our unconscious mind automatically internalizes and stores all this rich material and it becomes a sort of "blueprint" we build love on. The problem is that these patterns are natural and automatic and they're all we've known. Still most of us want more than the quality of love our parents had. Today for the first time in history we have the tools to be able to reprogram our patterns so love is more fulfilling and nourishing. We have more options today than simply settling, being roommates, having affairs, or divorce. We can invest in love and grow together to make our wonderful vision of heart-centered love a reality. Isn't love worth it?

CHANGE YOUR LEVEL OF LOVE, NOT YOUR PARTNER!

What if you could **grow with your partner** and gradually you could both begin to feel closer than you even dreamed of? Today this is possible if you invest some time and effort and both of you **stretch emotionally** and **open your hearts**. Let's face it, if you've lost the spark, if you feel shut down or turned off, if you have a wall that keeps you distant or superficial, your heart isn't as open to your partner as it could be. But what if you could **grow together** and, working as a team, you could begin to communicate in patterns that **feel more nurturing?** What if you started to support each other emotionally? If you both begin **to feel heard**, to have **empathy for each other**, you would feel closer. What if you could learn how to **increase emotional trust** together? What if you and your partner started to treat your relationship with more care, to be **more reciprocal** in nourishing each other. What if you brought **more energy, vitality and maturity** to each other? What if you learned how to have **healthier boundaries** and didn't feel controlled, enmeshed or drained by the relationship? When couples grow together they feel closer and more nourished. Gradually they want to be **"lovers"** again and feel **passion, desire and attraction** return. Yes it's possible but we aren't programmed for this level of love. Reprogramming is a series of steps and tools to guide you to open your heart to your partner all over again! It's worth some time and effort because love is an investment that always appreciates!

Welcome to the HIGHER LEVEL LOVE couples program.

Workbook 1-Growing Our Relationship Together

In order to make significant changes in how you approach each other emotionally, how you communicate, and how you relate to each other you have to begin grow out of patterns internalized from childhood, from your parents' personalities, and from how you were treated. To do this you have to take some steps before you can run! The first step is to change the way you look at love! Part One will help you both do that! You can use some tools to grow out of a lower level of love! You can have the level of love you've dreamed of, but no one is entitled to it. We are all growing into heart-centered love! Since we base our whole life on love, isn't it worth it to spend the time to raise your relationship to a higher level? Part one will help couples grow in the ways listed, using tools in a step by step program.

- We will begin to identify how we are stuck as a couple
- We will focus on how buried anger and anxiety gets triggered and causes many symptoms we suffer from
- We will begin to understand different levels of love and work together to grow to a higher level of love
- We will use tools to move out of blaming and stop being adversarial, to take down some of our "walls"
- We will learn tools to stop being distant as either "roommates" or by "acting out" anger and drama together
- We will rebuild emotional trust together and increase our capacity to "be there" for each other with more connection
- We will learn to allow feedback with each other so we can grow together and become more nourishing partners
- We will use some tools to give each other feedback about chores, money, romance, sexuality and other issues
- We will start to recognize how we live "in our head" and aren't able to connect emotionally to each other
- We will have a tool to practice empathy, support and have healthier, more open communication with each other
- We will be able to start to date like "lovers" again
- We will identify some core wounds in our personality that get triggered and interfere with love, are a burden on love
- We will identify problems that keep us at risk, attached at our weakest link instead of with the highest-functioning parts of our personalities, with our hearts

Workbook 1: Growing Our Relationship Together

	Steps to a higher level of love	Reprogramming Tools Exercises & Tools	What couples can begin to work on together	Our Homework
Week 1	Opening Up our relationship	• Tools not Talk! • Buried anger issues • Our relationship patterns-foundation • Levels of love chart • How are we stuck?	Tools will help us identify some common problems with communication, relationship patterns that keep love stuck, feeling stale, distant, with resentment causing "walls".	#1 Journaling a problem and talking about it together
Week 2	Moving out of "Blaming"	• Blaming issues keep us "adversarial" • The lowest level of love isn't nourishing • Why we can't talk! • Blaming is explained	Tools will guide us to be a team, not adversaries stuck in familiar power-struggles with nagging, bickering, and acting out anger at each other. We want to stop blaming and go forward.	#2 Journaling about how we become stuck when we're adversarial
Week 3	Taking Down our "Walls"	• Do we have "walls" • Being open enough for higher level love • Managing moods • Patterns build walls	Couples who feel like roommates or who act out anger don't feel "heard" or get their needs met. Negative moods can become a burden on a partner. This can cause emotional "walls".	#3 Journaling about our "walls" in more detail
Week 4	Our level of Emotional Trust	• Rebuild emotional trust together • Communication increases trust	We can increase the level of emotional trust we feel. Using some tools we can begin to "be there" and feel nourished.	#4 Journaling about our level of emotional trust
Week 5	Giving- Receiving Feedback	• Are you in your head- not in your heart? • Feedback deepens our communication • Do we act out anger • Sex, money, chores • Dating like lovers	Couples who stay on the surface feel distant and controlled and aren't open or connected enough to be close in healthy, nourishing ways. Feedback opens up our communication together.	#5 Journal about some things you avoid, take some risks and talk with more depth
Week 6	Communication- Feeling "Heard"	• Reflecting, Empathy, Support • Patterns that end communication	Practicing communication exercises at home helps us to show empathy and support.	#6 Journal about giving and getting feedback together
Week 7	Core wounds are Our Baggage	• Core Wounds get triggered • Our "baggage" • Our Weakest Link	When couples are attached with their baggage they act out core wounds together. This puts them at risk!	#7 Describe my 2-3 core wounds that interfere with our love
Week 8	Growing Together A more Heart-Centered love	• Lowest level of love • Couples using tools • We aren't entitled	We aren't entitled to a higher level of love but we can grow into it. We base our whole life on love. Isn't it worth it?	#8 Journal about what I want to grow and change

Workbook 1-GROWING OUR RELATIONSHIP TOGETHER

GROWING OUR RELATIONSHIP TOGETHER

HEART-CENTERED LOVE

PROGRAMMING
stuck in unhealthy
patterns

REPROGRAMMING
a higher level of
love

OPENING UP OUR RELATIONSHIP...

Week 1	Reprogramming Tools Exercises, Homework, Tools
Opening Up Our Relationship	• Tools not "talk"! Investing in Love • Buried anger issues need tools • Our Relationship Foundation-common patterns • LEVELS of LOVE chart • How are we stuck?

OPENING UP OUR RELATIONSHIP

Our first step in learning how to use tools is to be willing to open up our relationship and get to work! Pretending things are **fine and glossing over** real problems doesn't solve anything. It's natural to do that because we were taught to when we were children. It's okay **to deny and minimize issues** and problems if there isn't much you can do about them. This might have worked well in childhood when you didn't have much power to make significant changes. It isn't a good strategy for adult love relationships. In fact it makes problems worse over time. It causes those silent walls of emotional distance. It turns off passion and deadens desire. It keeps us **stuck "on the surface"** which isn't a very intimate and close relationship.

Sometimes couples are afraid to open up and admit to each other that they feel dissatisfied with their distance or that they have problems. It's fairly typical for **one partner to feel comfortable** with the way things are and for the other partner to want some growth. The partner who is the most **stuck and resistant** will tend to deny, gloss over and pretend things are fine. This partner may even **rationalize** things, "Everyone has problems.", "We don't have it so bad.", "Why make waves." This will keep you both stuck. Eventually this won't work and you may even have a **crisis of awakening** down the road to force you to open up. Why wait for that? If your partner won't make changes with you, don't stress about it. Do the program by yourself for awhile. Nothing will stay the same!

Buried feelings get stuck in our personality in core wounds that get triggered and cause some of our worse moods. We suffer from a lot of **symptoms of buried feelings**. Don't get hooked on antidepressants for years, open up your personality and release this old toxic material. Later on these tools will be discussed. Triggered moods and reactions that surface in love relationships often cause resentment and distance and make love feel tense. Identify some of your moods or triggers and see if your partner feels your negative reactions limit communication, put a damper on fun and romance, and feel like a burden on love.

Use the first homework journaling lesson to begin to talk with more focus. If your partner "ends the communication" by attacking, being defensive, with a counterattack, or some other way to keep communication on the surface, don't lose heart! You will get some tools for these problems soon. Here are some of the tools you will be using week by week in this program!

Tools for a more Heart-Centered Love

COMMUNICATION TOOLS
- **TOOLS TO FEEL HEARD, VALIDATE EACH OTHER**
- **EXERCISES TO INCREASE EMOTIONAL TRUST**
- **TOOLS TO BE MORE OF A TEAM TOGETHER**

TOOLS FOR EMOTIONAL DISTANCE
- **IDENTIFY PATTERNS THAT KEEP US DISTANT**
- **TOOLS TO STOP BEING "ADVERSARIAL"**
- **TOOLS TO CHANGE STAYING ON THE SURFACE**

TOOLS for HEALTHIER SEXUALITY
- **SEX WITHOUT A CONNECTION, AFFECTION**
- **A SEXUAL DEMAND FOR SEX AS A "FIX"**
- **STUCK IN UNHEALTHY PATTERNS SEXUALLY**

TOOLS FOR MATURE INTIMACY
- **LACK OF ENERGY FOR ROMANCE, FUN, PLAY**
- **BURIED FEELINGS CAUSE MOODS, LOW ENERGY**
- **BEGIN TO DATE LIKE "LOVERS" AGAIN**

TOOLS FOR BURIED ANGER
- **BURIED FEELINGS GET TRIGGERED AS MOODS**
- **ANGER CAUSES WALLS BETWEEN PARTNERS**
- **ANGER SURFACES FROM CORE WOUNDS**

One partner can make a difference- without your partner's permission or participation!

Your relationship growth is up to you and you can make changes with or without your partner! When one partner is actively doing the homework it is often inspiring and **motivates the other partner**. You can also motivate your partner by asking to do journaling together at one convenient time for 10 minutes, and then talking about your issues together. Your effort and commitment to your own growth and to the changes is necessary for the success you want to see in your relationship. Becoming open to changing your issues will help you grow to becoming a more heart-centered partner. **Heart-centered love** will nourish your life!

Your partner isn't holding you back! Remember **one partner** can change the whole relationship! If you change your patterns, the relationship dynamic will change and nothing can stay the same. You can grow out of your patterns, use your tools for more open communication, set healthier emotional boundaries, and use exercises to reprogram yourself for a heart-centered love. A higher level of love is more nourishing. **Even if your partner won't work** with you, you can change what you are frustrated with by working at these issues yourself. Many partners have done this with success.

You have chosen a unique, innovative, and progressive program to work with. As you do your share of homework exercises at home you will begin to notice some subtle differences. It will be gradual at first but just keep on, keeping on! As you use an "adult voice" and communicate in more open, inviting patterns things will change. Instead of being ignored for nagging or complaining you will be taken more seriously. You can set healthy, mature boundaries for dates, for affection, for support and companionship, and certainly for sex. **Changing how you stay enmeshed** in unhealthy patterns will move everything forward. The "dog whisperer" on TV has proven that old dogs can learn new tricks! We are not limited to the patterns our family background programmed us with. We can learn new patterns and reprogram how we relate to our partner. **We base our whole life on love** so it makes sense to commit to making it more fulfilling and nourishing!

Isn't love worth it?

Is Buried Anger or Old Pain a Problem?

Buried ANGER and PAIN is usually forgotten by the time you are an adult. It can get **triggered** over and over again causing many problems in adult relationships, even though you may not remember the cause. Buried pain is split off from everyday conscious awareness so **you don't feel it.** The problem is it keeps coming to the surface until it is healed. It doesn't go away by talking yourself out of it, avoiding it, talking "about it". You may not know it is there but **there are many symptoms** of buried pain and anger. √ Check those you want to grow out of. Cross out a part of a symptom that doesn't fit you (if most of it does fit) and check it anyway. Core wounds cause these symptoms!

[ ] My anger comes out in intense angry moods, road rage, irritability
[ ] I can't relax easily, stay compulsive and "busy", mind is "racing"
[ ] I feel pressure to "do something", have a "to do" list in my head
[ ] One part of me is critical, I never measure up, I beat myself up
[ ] I don't feel "safe", feel like "something bad is going to happen"
[ ] I don't trust people, keep a guard up, feel people will be critical
[ ] I have an addiction, it's caused by buried pain and anger
[ ] I have compulsive behaviors, habits that I feel controlled by
[ ] I eat compulsively, have an eating disorder or body image issues
[ ] I have sleep problems due to anxiety, stress, can't let go
[ ] I worry, overplan, overthink , tend to watch, "observe" myself
[ ] I feel disconnected, "OK, Fine, Up, On", I have to be strong
[ ] I caretake others, do it all, tend to be in control, don't lean much
[ ] I change to a younger, childlike personality around my partner
[ ] I feel like "something is missing" in my adult life, I'm bored, stuck
[ ] I have depression that keeps re-cycling, can't seem to get rid of it
[ ] I have migraines, physical problems, feel tense, stressed out a lot
[ ] I can't remember chunks of the past, tend to deny/avoid feelings
[ ] I have to "have fun" to feel alive, I need danger, adrenaline high
[ ] I get tired of one partner quickly, fantasize, can't get really close
[ ] I can't get angry, can't say no, don't feel much personal power
[ ] I feel something inside sabotages success, holds me back
[ ] I feel tired, empty without my partner, lonely by myself
[ ] I focus on my relationship, not on my own life, I don't have goals
[ ] I feel afraid, anxious, stressed, frantic, overwhelmed too often
[ ] My life feels like it's hard, not easy, like a struggle, is crisis to crisis
[ ] My moods control me, I can't manage my emotional reactions
[ ] I feel too much dependency with a parent, don't feel separate
[ ] I live "in my head", I feel like I'm going through the motions a lot
[ ] I feel too serious, responsible, it's hard to "play", feel free, have fun
[ ] I don't enjoy sex, don't feel very sexually attracted to my partner
[ ] I feel insecure, "not good enough", compare myself to others
[ ] My life feels like it's a treadmill, I can't slow down, I'm always busy

Name_____ Date_____

Compulsive and Addictive Issues
Interfere with Love

Compulsive issues really start in childhood and have to do with **staying disconnected** from buried feelings, feelings that were too uncomfortable to feel a long time ago. Staying **compulsively busy**, having to be with other people compulsively, avoiding your own company and time alone to recharge yourself, can be subtle and insidious. Without even realizing it you may avoid your feelings by getting on the internet, making some calls, or watching TV too much. Never have any down time, just you and you? This can actually interfere with love going to a higher level. Healthy love has to do with your capacity for **authentic emotional connection** to your feelings, not just the "needy" ones we all feel. All relationships have some anger to deal with, some of those times where partners disagree and have to be able to talk about it. People with compulsive issues **skim along on the surface** and can't make deeper connections. They are **usually "in their head"**, analyzing and controlling everything: but mostly their emotional reactions. They don't react from the depth of their heart and they can't make a deep emotional connection most of the time. To be in a relationship with a partner with compulsive issues you will have to tolerate a certain degree of distance. Some couples say they feel like roommates. Other couples can't deal with the feelings they stuff so feelings build up until **they explode** in a mood of anxiety, depression, anger, or more compulsiveness. Compulsive issues keep love stuck! Often compulsive issues appear as codependency, taking care of others, focusing on others and their problems. It's important to use tools to "get out of your head" and connect deep enough for a higher level of love. Compulsive issues **keep you busy but not nourished.**

We all know **addictions interfere with healthy love**. Addictions, just like compulsive issues, have to do with buried feelings that cause moods. You don't feel them anymore, but **you feel the symptoms**: being too wound up inside, having anxiety that won't resolve, feeling angry or irritated, impatient, stressed causes the uncomfortable, disconnected feelings of unrest that leads **to the next fix for the "inner addict".** Did you know that we all have an inner addict, called the wounded child inside of us? The inner addict has learned how to make a habit that causes it to be able to avoid feeling the unrest that goes along with buried feelings. After a few years the habit itself is pleasurable and becomes a goal in itself. Can we change our habits? Absolutely! The tools for a higher level of love also help you have a healthier lifestyle. As you learn how to **bring the highest-functioning part of your personality** to your relationship and use it to grow out of unhealthy dependency, you will also have tools for your lifestyle changes. Addictions keep relationships unsatisfying, unhealthy, and troubled.

Healthy lifestyles are a foundation to build love on!

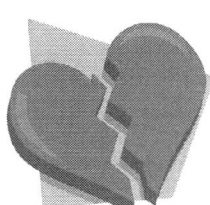

Our Relationship Foundation

COMMON BOUNDARY & COMMUNICATION ISSUES
THAT CAUSE A LOWER LEVEL OF LOVE!

COMMUNICATION ISSUES

[ ]I avoid discussing problems, there just isn't time, it wouldn't help anyway
[ ]I bring up all the issues and have to force my partner to talk about issues
[ ]I tend to be "right", to quote authorities, to be verbal and articulate
[ ]I shut down, give up, give in, just let things go, and don't get ruffled much anyway
[ ]I tend to think things are fine, OK, am not in touch with feelings very much
[ ]My partner is too controlling sometimes, I can't just "be me"
[ ]I can ramble, lecture, be a bit of a "know-it-all", feel life has a lot of "rules"/ "shoulds"
[ ]I can end the conversation by avoiding, attacking, accusing, changing the subject
[ ]What problems? My partner is the one with all the problems, it's his/her fault
[ ]No one really "gets in" or gets very close to me, I am in control, have a "wall" up

BOUNDARIES AND CODEPENDENCY ISSUES

[ ]I feel my partner is too controlling, bossy, makes me feel like a "child" in some ways
[ ]I have built my life around my partner, I focus a lot of my attention on trying to get intimacy/affection/time with my partner, I can be moody when I don't get enough
[ ]I expect my partner to call or report in, if we're apart I feel kind of bored, moody
[ ]My partner is my "best friend", I don't need anyone else
[ ]I want some space with my partner, feel "smothered",controlled in some ways
[ ]I wish my partner had some friends, activities, a group, goals, instead of just "me"
[ ]I feel anxious, uncomfortable, can't relax if my partner is moody and have to "fix it"
[ ]I am a "pleaser", I try to do whatever my partner wants, I pamper my partner
[ ]I feel taken for granted, even "used", but I like being needed by my partner
[ ]I can be a little demanding and expect a bit of pampering from my partner
[ ]I "act out" my moods in my relationship: get angry and start a fight with my partner, blow up, nitpick/criticize to get attention, am moody/sullen/ melancholy need to be cheered up, or anxious/worry/ stressed, am in pain or feel sick a lot
[ ]I do too much of the responsibilities in our relationship, we don't share the burden
[ ]I can be too rigid, try to "mold" my partner to be what I want, I can be controlling

FAMILY ISSUES

[ ]I am overly involved with a child, he/she is my "best friend", I focus on him/her a lot
[ ]Family relationships are an issue in our relationship, we need to improve this area
[ ]We fight about family issues, focus on family problems instead of our own issues
[ ]One or both of us is too dependent on our family, are not separate whole adults
[ ]Instead of being close to each other, one of us is too emotionally attached to family
[ ]We are not a team with our family issues, blended family, relatives

Name_____ Date_____

CLOSENESS AND DISTANCE ISSUES

[ ]We are too distant, live like roommates, we lack romance or passion between us
[ ]I manage my feelings and moods with drugs or alcohol and keep my distance
[ ]My relationship has power-struggles, is tense, has a "wall" between us
[ ]My relationship lacks mature romance and an adult sexual relationship, we have
      mechanical sex just to connect, sex is the main way we feel close
[ ]I am too insecure, jealous, possessive, anxious about my partner leaving me or
      cheating and don't feel close unless I control my partner
[ ]We are good companions but we can't "talk" about us, our issues, problems
[ ]We fight a lot instead of talk, get close, feel affectionate: there's always something
[ ]We have a push-pull pattern of closeness, get close after a fight, one of us
       threatens to leave, has one foot out the door sometime, we are on the brink a lot
[ ]My partner blames most of our issues on me, doesn't seem to look at his/her part
[ ]My partner has to be right, "makes me wrong", tells me what's wrong with me
[ ]The only way to be close to my partner is to do what he/she wants
[ ]We aren't a team solving problems together, we try to make the other one wrong
[ ]I feel nothing I do is good enough for my partner, he/she is very critical
[ ]My partner's addictions are what our life centers around, taking care of problems
[ ]My partner gives money instead of intimacy and I want more of a real relationship
[ ]We live in a state of chaos, turmoil, drama, crisis and are just trying to survive

ROMANCE AND SEXUALITY ISSUES

[ ]We aren't romantic, don't make time for "dates" together, are comfortable but bored
[ ]Sex feels like a chore to one or both of us, is mechanical, lacks passion, excitement
[ ]There are other problems that effect our sex life: depression, resentments, lack of
      closeness, or (describe):_____
[ ]My partner doesn't want to improve our sex life, won't admit there is a problem
[ ]My partner is withholding sexually, refuses to have sex without a fight, ultimatum
[ ]My partner has a "sexual demand" for sex , expects sex often or almost daily,
      gets moody, threatens to cheat on me, gets mad, needs sex to feel OK , I feel
      pressure to meet my partner's needs, my needs get pushed aside and ignored
[ ]We don't really have much fun together because my partner doesn't try to be fun
      (describe): _____
[ ]My partner does not plan romantic dates, initiate sex, cuddle, act sensual
[ ]My partner shuts me out sexually

FINANCES, CHORES, AND RESPONSIBILITES ISSUES

[ ]We don't share our chores in a flowing way, one is "the boss", other is "the kid"
[ ]We don't have a plan for sharing finances as a couple, one partner runs the show,
      makes decisions, controls the purse-strings, hands out the money
[ ]We argue about money, don't set goals and live on a reasonable budget
[ ]We have too much clutter, mess, don't work together at having a comfortable space
[ ]One partner does most of the "work", feels burdened, chores aren't shared
[ ]My partner only helps out if I prod, remind, nag and tell him/her what to do each time
[ ]My partner says "yes" but then "forgets", has excuses, only helps out for a few days
[ ]My partner "forgets" to pay bills, spends impulsively, will spend more than we have
[ ]I can't win, either I nag or get ignored, my partner acts like a child with me

MOVING TO A HIGHER LEVEL OF LOVE!

Higher Love  **Has a Heart Connection!**	**A MORE NOURISHING LEVEL OF LOVE** • both take more responsibility • love feels fun, more alive, closer • emotional trust is higher now • communication is open, deeper • they feel more nourished by each other, more supported • their foundation is healthier • the highest-functioning parts of each partner are connected and they feel more attracted	-stale walls" of silent distance are removed, healed -relationship feels open, nourishing, has more passion -both use tools to create a healthier level of love -they now approach each other with a "heart" connection
Being a team Together  **Love doesn't feel so stuck**	**STARTING TO GROW** • they begin to talk more openly and start to really feel heard • their connection gets deeper • partners begin to feel less controlled, react less controlling • as couples start to have more fun, closeness they feel more desire, attraction for each other • stop blaming, being adversaries • use **TOOLS** to shift out of their emotional baggage, the moods, reactions that keep them stuck • approach each other with their highest functioning parts	-they have moved out of "blaming" patterns - emotional trust gradually increases -they each begin to "own" some of the responsibility -are more emotionally available and open -use tools to shift into healthier, and highest functioning parts of themselves
Love is at risk!  **Lowest level of "love" isn't satisfying**	**PATTERNS CAUSE LOVE TO FEEL STUCK!** • They can't "talk" together • fight or stay superficial, closed • they give in, give up, withdraw • they feel controlled, controlling • aren't mature, healthy lovers • they both blame each other • they have low emotional trust • don't feel nourished, full • these partners are attached with the most immature, wounded parts of each other	-partners are unaware of real issues, just anger, not what causes it -they "act out" their emotional baggage with each other automatically -they are stuck "blaming", and both feel distant, resentful -they can't connect with the highest-functioning parts of themselves

Raising the level of our Love!

OPENING UP OUR COMMUNICATION
[ ] we want our communication to be more open, to have depth
[ ] we want to "be heard" by each other in order to feel closer
[ ] we want tools to be able to talk about our relationship problems
[ ] we want to be able to disagree without drama and anger
[ ] we want to talk so our communication doesn't end or escalate

INCREASING OUR EMOTIONAL TRUST
[ ] we need to be able to show that we care how each other feels, what the
    other needs emotionally and that it's important, it matters
[ ] we need to have empathy for the way our partner is feeling with us
[ ] we want to be emotionally trusted and act with integrity together
[ ] we want to take care of each other's needs in healthy ways (a relationship
    isn't exploitive, "me, me, me", my way)
[ ] we want to improve emotional trust so we both feel that we're really
    "there" for each other with support, caring, empathy

GROWING INTO A HEALTHIER DEPENDENCY
[ ] we both want to work at having healthy lifestyles with friends, interests,
    goals, dreams; our relationship isn't a hide-out or a crutch
[ ] we are in therapy or recovery if we need tools to deal issues that impact
    our relationship (addictions, compulsive issues)
[ ] we want to bring energy and vitality to our relationship so it thrives
[ ] we want tools to manage our moods, our "baggage" so we aren't a burden
    on our relationship or drain on each other emotionally
[ ] we want to grow out of codependent-dependent patterns that cause
    resentment and "walls", keeping us distant and stuck

IMPROVING SEXUAL ISSUES-INCREASING DESIRE
[ ] we want more emotional connection, closeness when we have sex
[ ] we want to feel close, warm, cared for, nourished sexually
[ ] we want to stop having sex from guilt, pressure, obligation
[ ] we want sex to have a more open, fun, passionate, giving feeling
[ ] we want more flirting, desire and attraction again like we once felt

We want a HIGHER LEVEL of LOVE!

Name_____ Date_____

Is our relationship STUCK?

COMMUNICATION

[ ] We avoid discussing our real problems in a deep, problem-solving fashion. We rarely discuss the real issues. We tend to stay on the surface so we feel comfortable, keep the peace. We often pretend things are "fine" or just ignore them.

[ ] We tend to bicker, nag, complain, and blame each other a lot. We don't discuss our feelings and needs in ways that cause real changes. We end up back where we started. We don't see our own part in the problems, what our patterns are.

[ ] We have fights but one of us has to give in just to make peace. We don't resolve our differences, we stuff them and pretend to be ok with it, to make peace. One person wins, one loses. Nothing much changes.

[ ] In our relationship we can't communicate effectively because we aren't two "equals". One of us is more passive, withdraws, gives in, or shuts down while the other partner seems to have more power or is more opinionated, will speak up more.

NURTURANCE, WARMTH, SUPPORT

[ ] We often feel we don't get our needs met. There is not enough affection, support, or genuine "giving" to make the relationship very close. One partner is too needy, the other too distant or withholds affection, sex.

[ ] We feel too distant, too disconnected, like we're going through the motions, doing the same old boring things together. We rarely have adult fun or romance together. We have a silent "wall" between us.

[ ] We don't know how to nurture each other in warm, mature ways. We tend to "act out" our needs instead, often with anger, guilt, by being demanding, pressuring, with threats or ultimatums. This is also a turn off sexually.

[ ] One partner tends to act superior, righteous, like he/she knows the right way, may preach or lecture, teach . The other partner may feel belittled, talked down to, or patronized, trivialized. It can feel like a parent-child relationship in ways.

SEXUALITY

[ ] Our sex life is unsatisfying, sometimes it's one-sided. There is a lack of passion. Sex can feel like an obligation, a chore. The partner who wants it will pout, pressure, use guilt or get mad until his/her needs are met.

[ ] In some ways sex is about a "fix" rather than adult closeness, affection, warmth, loving. There's an unspoken expectation, a pressure for sex. It's the main way we get close, but there's not much romance, flirting, foreplay, adult fun in our sex life.

[ ] We feel more like best friends or partners than lovers. If we have sex we aren't into it, passionate and affectionate. We have tension about sex underneath the surface.

Name_____   Date_____

Just 10 minutes! Isn't love worth it?

Journaling improves Communication!

*Set a timer for 10 minutes. Journal together as a couple for just 10 minutes! Write out **your feelings about your relationship.** It will help you focus and organize your thoughts so you can be "heard". Then set the timer for another 5 minutes for each person and listen to your partner talk, without arguing or interrupting, getting defensive. This is an important step in beginning to be more open together. Research has found journaling improves communication. Sometimes it takes practice to "get out of your head" and really get a focus and learn how to have a voice and feel heard.

USING JOURNALING
TO OPEN UP OUR RELATIONSHIP

Describe a relationship problem that is important to work on. Give some background and examples. Only write for 10 minutes and then talk together.

Name_____   Date_____

GROWING OUR RELATIONSHIP TOGETHER

PROGRAMMING
stuck in unhealthy patterns

HEART-CENTERED LOVE

REPROGRAMMING
a higher level of love

MOVING OUT OF "BLAMING"!

Week 2	Reprogramming Tools Exercises, Homework and Tools
Moving out of Blaming	• **Blaming issues keep us "adversarial"** • **The lowest level of love isn't nourishing** • **Why we can't talk!** • **Blaming is explained**

WE NEED TOOLS TO STOP BLAMING!

Most couples are blaming because they feel frustrated. This is perfectly natural but it's only a problem because you can't move forward. Blaming can be a way to listen to your frustration, to point to a problem, and to notice your feelings. So go ahead and blame but **don't get stuck** and stay there. When you journal and notice yourself feeling resentful and blaming, pause it, and you'll learn how to use a tool to do something proactive! This is just the beginning. It's sort of like getting fed up with your weight and blaming food, lack of exercise, and so on. A good first step, it points you in a direction, but it isn't going to take the pounds off! There's nothing wrong with blaming unless you get stuck and feel like a nag, keep venting your anger in predictable irritable moods, and make the same old half-hearted, empty promises. Blaming won't move you forward. It's actually immature to stay stuck in it. It **becomes an excuse** for venting, name-calling, and abuse. Week by week you will get tools to help you move out of blaming.

Partners who are stuck in blaming feel **adversarial.** As soon as you're in an adversarial position with each other, you aren't being a team. Your anger will escalate and nothing much will get accomplished. Sometimes when we are **clogged up with buried feelings** (old anger or anxiety) we actually **pick fights and needle** each other to be able to "get it out". Over time this will damage a relationship and you won't feel better anyway. If you begin to notice that you're adversarial with each other, you aren't going to get much accomplished when you talk, you **won't resolve problems.** Being adversarial makes you feel like your partner **"isn't there for you"** in important ways. Ironically both partners feel this. Most of us fight over everyday things that are actually fairly mundane. What's really going on is we want to **"be heard."** As soon as you become adversarial with each other you aren't there for your partner. No one really feels heard.

The **lowest level of love** is what most people experience at some time in our life. Love gets stuck in **emotional ruts.** It doesn't fulfill our needs and usually there's some emotional distance. Some couples describe it as **"roommates" and others bicker and have power-struggles** over everyday things. The lowest level of love is common but it isn't satisfying. It has communication issues, and the emotional distance causes passion and desire to dwindle. Partners don't feel taken seriously, probably have a "wall" or stay on the surface too much. These are just some of the symptoms of love at this level, but not the causes. Our parents often had this level of love and there just wasn't a lot they could do about it. Today we have tools to **raise love to a more open and nourishing level**. We don't have to settle or tolerate this level of love. We can raise it to a more intimate level!

ARE WE TOO "ADVERSARIAL"?
My partner doesn't feel like "my friend"!
We are either "roommates" or feel tense!

[   ] We tend to work against each other, not with each other

[   ] We don't feel like a "team" making decisions jointly, easy

[   ] One or both of us "builds a case" to be right, justifies, defends

[   ] We feel resentment toward each other, stay "roommates"

[   ] One partner takes an "innocent/righteous" stance

[   ] We feel stuck "blaming" each other, can't move forward

[   ] One partner has to give in, be quiet, give up, or stuff it

[   ] One of us will pout, sulk, punish, be moody, threaten

[   ] We don't compromise, negotiate on everyday decisions

[   ] I don't feel "heard", my feelings don't seem important

[   ] I feel powerless in some ways with this partner, a "victim"

Are we stuck at the lowest Level of Love?

- Relationships feel stuck at this level, aren't fulfilling or nourishing
- Partners can't resolve their issues with open communication
- Sex lacks passion and desire caused by "walls" of distance
- Partners have poor emotional boundaries, are reactive, can't talk
- Underlying resentments surfaces as "triggered" anger
- A feeling of tension, strain is often present or we are "roommates"
- Emotional trust is low, relationship may be exploitive, dishonest
- The relationship feels adversarial, has power-struggles
- Partners don't take much responsibility for the relationship

---

Journal about a problem area that you feel is a focus for couples growth. Do you begin to feel "adversarial" , argumentative , or blaming instead of being supportive, cooperative, a team, on the same side!

- Give examples of how **communication ends** when we try to talk.
- Being **adversarial, argumentative and blaming** keeps us stuck.
- When the communication ends we **can't resolve issues** when we talk. We just give up or give in.

Hint: When we become "adversarial" , we aren't a team about working toward a solution. We just try to **build a case, make each other wrong.** It's a **power-struggle.** We push each other away instead of compromise and cooperate. This isn't supportive!

Journal about an issue, problem or feelings we become argumentative, blaming or adversarial about. Who becomes defensive, who is blaming and who uses anger to control the flow? This stops communication dead in its tracks! What is a difficult problem area to try to talk about? Why?

We get stuck when we try to talk about...

Name_____ Date_____

The Lowest Level of Love
EMOTIONAL DISTANCE KEEPS US STUCK!

Nothing I do is ever enough!

You're too defensive! I don't feel heard!

I'm fed up with trying so hard!

You try to control me, not nurture me!

You blame it all on me! You think you're a victim.

You want sex without real connection or romance.

> **WE'RE ATTACHED at our WEAKEST LINK!**

- WE DON'T TRUST EACH OTHER TO "BE THERE" FOR EACH OTHER EMOTIONALLY. WE DON'T "FEEL HEARD".

- NEGATIVE MOODS ARE AN EMOTIONAL BURDEN THAT CAUSES A "WALL" OF RESENTENT BETWEEN US.

- WE BOTH SILENTLY BLAME EACH OTHER FOR WHY WE FEEL UNFULFILLED AND STAY DISTANT.

- UNHEALTHY DEPENDENCY AND CODEPENDENCY PATTERNS KEEP US TOO ENMESHED (I CAN'T "BE ME").

- WE BLAME, FIGHT, COMPLAIN, OR NAG BUT WE CAN'T COMMUNICATE DEEPLY AND RESOLVE PROBLEMS.

- WE FEEL LIKE "ADVERSARIES", AND HAVE POWER-STRUGGLES INSTEAD OF BEING A TEAM TOGETHER.

- WE HAVE DESIRE AND ATTRACTION PROBLEMS, OR FEEL SEX IS A PRESSURE, AN UNSPOKEN DEMAND FOR A FIX.

- ONE PARTNER IS OFTEN DEMANDING (entitled)–WHILE THE OTHER PARTNER IS OFTEN PLEASING (caretaking)

The Lowest Level of Love

- **Communication issues, Resentments**

- **Emotional Trust, Empathy are low**

- **Emotional Needs aren't being met**

- **Emotional Distance and Abuse**

- **Sexual Distance, loss of Desire**

- **Unhealthy Dependency issues**

- **Codependency and Boundary issues**

COUPLES AT RISK!

Moving out of "BLAMING"

[   ] We feel like **we are being "adversaries"**, not on the same team, being supportive of each other and compromising together.

[   ] We have "low emotional trust" with each other because **we aren't "there" for each other**, don't hear each other, don't validate each other.

[   ] To increase our level of emotional trust, we both need to learn how take our own share, **our 50% each, of the responsibility** for our relationship problems.

[   ] We get angry over small things, it escalates too fast, and we get "triggered" sometimes. We have **a wall between us because of blaming**.

[   ] We have **power-struggles, bicker, nag** or tend to complain about too many things, and one of us shuts down or gives in to keep peace.

[   ] We **aren't affectionate physically** with each other and we don't hug, cuddle, caress, give each other much physical tenderness, gentleness, sensuality.

The good news is you can change this!

MOVE OUT OF "BLAMING"!
Does Blaming keep our
Relationship Stuck!

"Blaming" just keeps you both Angry!

[   ] Do you "build a case" and find evidence to "be right"? Do you tend to see your partner as "the problem" and feel "innocent" or taken advantage of?

[   ] Do you and your partner feel like you're on "opposite sides, like adversaries who make each other wrong" instead of being able to resolve issues?

[   ] Do you hang on to "old grudges" and bring them up as a reason to stay angry and resentful instead of looking at the whole picture and getting past them?

[   ] Does anger keep your relationship emotionally distant? When your partner wants to try to resolve things do you sabotage it by pointing the finger?

[   ] Do you recognize your 50% of the problems, and do you bring it up and "own it" so you can move forward? Do you try to change your issues?

[   ] Do you spend a lot of time complaining about what is wrong? Do you take steps to change things other than just "talking" or having a fight?

[   ] Do you take the initiative to bring some healthy warm energy to your partner and your relationship? Do you plan dates and special alone time together?

[   ] Do you listen to constructive feedback about your part of the issues and take some responsibility for how your partner feels? Do you ask for feedback?

[   ] Do you use your anger as a righteous excuse to stay stuck, to drink, to use drugs, to flirt or cheat? Are you exploitive and self-absorbed? Are you emotionally selfish?

[   ] Are you passive and withdrawn (shut down) in your relationship instead of being a reciprocal partner? This will keep your relationship from growing to a higher level.

[   ] Does your partner complain that he/she can't "get in" with you? Are you closed, argumentative, controlling? Do you minimize, avoid problems or deny them?

[   ] Do you consistently look at what your partner is doing wrong but have a quick answer, a ready excuse, or an empty promise for your part of the issues?

Name_____   Date_____

Why can't we "talk" openly?

[   ] My partner has to be "right", doesn't listen to my side and I don't think I can be "heard" so I just shut up. We are too argumentative.

[   ] My partner "rambles" and goes on and on with too many details and we can't make headway. The subject loses focus or changes.

[   ] My partner "acts innocent" and doesn't take a real share, 50% of the responsibility for why we aren't close. We are stuck in blaming.

[   ] We have sexual issues and a problem with desire that keeps us from being attracted to each other. Our sex life is needy or one-sided.

[   ] We don't have any real "dates" with mature energy, fun, flirting and real closeness and connection. We don't feel like "lovers".

[   ] I feel like I am in my partner's shadow, and I am often an audience listening to my partner's accomplishments. I feel used emotionally.

[   ] My partner just keeps nitpicking and finding reasons to stay stuck and angry so we aren't close. I can't win. We are adversarial.

[   ] My partner is an "emotional bully" in some ways and keeps me "on edge". I can't feel relaxed, natural, be "me". I need healthy boundaries.

[   ] My partner has anger or depression problems that get in the way of us being a closer couple. There's always "something" to get mad about!

[   ] I feel like a child being lectured to. I am not taken very seriously and can't get my point across. I feel talked down to and bossed around.

[   ] It's all about what my partner needs and feels and how I am not taking care of my partner in "good enough" ways.   It's not reciprocal.

[   ] We can't really "talk" because there isn't much healthy motivation to make changes. Our lifestyle is too unhealthy for real growth.

Name_____   Date_____

Moving out of BLAMING!

- **I feel entitled to blame you because I'm RIGHT!**
- **I "build a case", I'm righteous! I can prove I'm right!**
- **I don't focus on my own 50% (my part) of the issues!**

You are being closed, demanding, and controlling by taking this attitude. These patterns are fairly rigid. You will just stay angry, nothing will change, and you will keep your partner at "arm's length" instead of solving issues and growing out of them. You aren't being open to a more mature, healthy closeness. This attitude ends the conversation and nothing can move forward. This will keep you stuck. You aren't approaching your partner from a healthy enough position to find solutions, meet your partner halfway, take your part of the responsibility. This isn't being a nourishing partner. You are undoubtedly "right" about some of these issues and your feelings, but aren't seeing the big picture, aren't being open to compromise, to being a team. This is called an **adversarial position**: you are against each other, blaming, pointing the finger. You need to take some responsibility for your part, for healthy boundaries on what you want and need. Moving out of this rigid, blaming, closed attitude will allow you to take responsibility, work as a team, compromise, and grow.

- **I nag, whine, or make you feel guilty for hurting me.**
- **I TRY TOO HARD but it's not ever enough! Poor me!**
- **I have no power with you, I'm not taken seriously.**

Whining, complaining, nagging, bitching is not attractive and you are confusing being needy with healthy mature love. You are in a "victim" position, feeling justified, **"innocent", and a little righteous** in your innocence. This position will keep you stuck blaming it all on your big, mean, bully of a partner who just won't take care of you in "good enough" ways. Staying resentful and angry in silent, submissive, passive ways isn't really being open. This will keep you angry, nothing will change, and you will keep your partner at "arm's length". You are not approaching your partner from a healthy enough position to be nourishing to your partner. You are "shut down" and reacting "in your head" without real awareness of how to take your own responsibility, set boundaries without anger, be inviting to your partner, and work as a team to find solutions. You are undoubtedly "right" about some of the issues and your feelings, but are not expressing them with your more mature "adult voice" (this is a tool) with healthy boundaries. This position is stuck, childish, and pointless. This is a programmed position that is immature.

- **I have a lot of good excuses for being so MOODY.**

- **My lifestyle is boring, draining, isn't fun, it's empty .**

- **I'm just tired, too busy, overwhelmed, or even feel sick!**

Approaching your partner from a closed position, with so little energy and vitality isn't nourishing your relationship. Being a couch potato doesn't have much vitality and both men and women do this. You may tend to whine, pout, complain, gripe about your aches and pains and get in angry moods at times. This is not healthy dependency. You may be confusing being needy with mature love, and feel entitled to "act out" stress, depression, and other moods that drain your relationship. Keeping **your lifestyle unhealthy**, too stressed or isolated and empty isn't bringing the energy, passion, vitality that couples with rich, full lifestyles have. This is a lifestyle issue. Your partner isn't supposed to be your whole world. The more you stay empty, tired, drained, and stressed the less you have to give to a relationship. Two empties don't make a whole! Because you aren't bringing much maturity and vitality to your partner, your partner will feel less attracted to you. Your lifestyle needs to fill you up, so you aren't stuck blaming your partner for being distant.

- **I take care of everyone and do it all, I'm so STRESSED!**

- **I feel in crisis and might get angry! I'm overwhelmed!**

- **I fill all my time with things that keep me very busy.**

This is a codependent pattern that causes you to have too much stress and to stay disconnected, detached from yourself emotionally, just running on empty! Your life isn't rich and full with real vitality. Both men and women do this. Buried anger, anxiety, emptiness from childhood often causes these patterns of staying compulsively driven to be busy and unable to slow down. You want to be taken care of in return for having dependent people need you. You aren't bringing real energy to your partner. You will tend to whine, pout, complain, and get angry at times or just be **on the surface emotionally** unable to let anyone really "in". You confuse being "needy-needed" with mature love, and feel entitled to "act out" your moods. You keep your lifestyle unhealthy, stressed or in crisis. No one gets very close to you, they only get close to the caretaker part of you. You keep your partner at "arm's length". Staying compulsively busy keeps you "shut down" and "in your head." This pattern keeps you emotionally unavailable. Blaming your partner isn't the answer.

GROWING OUR RELATIONSHIP TOGETHER

PROGRAMMING
stuck in unhealthy patterns

HEART-CENTERED LOVE

REPROGRAMMING
a higher level of love

TAKING DOWN OUR "WALLS"!

Week 3	Reprogramming Tools Exercises, Homework and Tools
Taking Down our "walls"	• Our "walls": roommates couples and couples who "act out" anger • Am I open enough for love? • Managing my moods • Patterns build "walls"-keep us distant

Taking Down Our Walls

It's not unusual for couples to develop some resentments over time. It would be strange if they didn't. People aren't perfect and neither are relationships. What causes a wall is when resentments aren't cleared up. When couples have faulty communication patterns they may unwittingly end the flow, stifle a partner, or even control the communication. Some couples keep the peace by **staying "on the surface"** and quietly rationalizing their real feelings away. Once in a while this is ok. But it is unhealthy for love when it happens most of the time. Couples stop feeling like "lovers". Some partners think because they have emotional meltdowns that they are being open and intimate with their feelings. If that was true, why doesn't it solve relationship problems? Being needy and having a meltdown in order to try to "be heard" is a sign you probably stay on the surface too much. When partners can't communicate with depth and the communication isn't open, eventually someone blows up or has a crisis. This is not the same thing as healthy intimate communication. Any 14 year old communicates this way! We are confused about what communication should look like! If your communication isn't causing you and your partner to feel closer and more loving you probably have a wall. We just aren't taught much about communication and suddenly we're in a relationship and it isn't working. We probably didn't have role models. We become close and feel like "lovers" when we feel supported, heard, validated and understood. When we **stay superficial or "on the surface"** we aren't intimate or connected deep enough to feel like "lovers". We may have lots of needy sex but that isn't the same thing. We're supposed to stay on the surface with acquaintances or people we keep at "arm's length", but not with our partner. If we have a pattern of being "in our head" too much we will tend to keep everyone in our life at a distance. This causes a wall.

Some partners **aren't emotionally open enough** for a higher level of love. This is caused by staying **compulsively busy**, one of the deadly sins of modern life. Some people idealize it and think it's a way to have power and feel important but it doesn't nourish anyone. Children of women who are detached, live "in their head", stay **compulsively "running on empty"** often feel anxious and deprived. They aren't emotionally nourished. Neither is their relationship. It isn't good for love, for your health, for your nerves, and it causes a wall.

ARE WE STUCK AT A LOWER LEVEL OF LOVE?

"ROOMMATES" COUPLE

They feel Comfortable with Emotional Distance

"ACTING OUT" COUPLE

Their Anger & Drama Creates Emotional Distance

ASEXUAL, lacks passion One/ both partners are shut down in their sexuality; one may be demanding sexually; sex may feel like a chore, an obligation, or feel pressured; one partner may avoid sex or try to get it over with	**EMOTIONAL DRAMA-ABUSE** This relationship is often intense due to strong emotional reactions and triggers; both partners "act out" core (childhood) wounds with buried anger, anxiety, or insecurity, or pain; drama causes abuse
BEST FRIENDS, comfortable Partners feel easy, comfortable but they aren't romantic/lovers; they may feel routine or boring; partners settle for companionship and emotional security without the depth of a healthier level of love	**ADVERSARIAL, not a team** This couple is not a team together; they fight, struggle rather than compromise; they don't support each other; they often push each other away emotionally; relationship has power-struggles and they both "blame" each other
EMOTIONAL DISTANCE This "best friends" relationship is built around chores, kids, family; each partner feels somewhat "alone" and disconnected in this kind of relationship; it can look good superficially; partners may stay together for appearances, but feel they are "settling"	**An INTENSE ATTACHMENT** Intense feelings are based on their dependency-codependency issues; they fight, have a lot of drama, crises; drama can be an excuse for addiction, staying compulsive, stuck; the relationship is draining, doesn't support their growth
AGREE not to DISAGREE Partners tend to stay busy, in their own worlds; avoid real issues; stuff/ignore feelings; both may try not to need much; they try not to rock the boat	**EMOTIONAL ABUSE** Partners emotionally abuse each other, often without much awareness; they have poor emotional boundaries; act out anger, are reactive, trigger each other easily
"SOMETHING IS MISSING" They may accept, rationalize their distance; partners aren't connected deeply; live "in their heads"; lack passion; tell themselves this is "all there is"; they feel "something is missing", but aren't attracted to each other enough to change	**ANGER BUILDS "WALLS"** Both partners are guarded; each partner blames the other for the problems, for their resentments, anger; may have little insight into issues; both get triggered and act out together; they have a "wall", stay on the surface
AVOID A DEEPER INTIMACY Partners tend to deny, avoid, or ignore deeper feelings, needs; rationalize them away; stay in control being busy or addictions, distractions, compulsive hobbies; they tolerate emotional distance	**PUSH-PULL DISTANCE** Partners use anger/drama to maintain an emotional distance; push each other away, then pull each other back with promises, temporary good behavior; real changes aren't lasting

Do we stay distant or superficial emotionally?
Is our relationship stuck?

Roommates Issues

[ ] We lack passion in our sexual intimacy. We feel comfortable but we aren't like "lovers". We date to do something, just to go out. It's ok but sort of ho-hum.

[ ] We are comfortable "best friends" but we aren't romantic, we don't attract each other as "lovers". We may feel bored, irritated with each other or stay superficial.

[ ] We stay emotionally distant and "on the surface" a lot of the time. We talk about chores, kids, current stuff, our responsibilities. We may take each other for granted.

[ ] We both try not to argue, we "fix it" if we do, we don't feel it's ok for the other partner to get mad. We keep the peace, give in. We don't want to make waves.

[ ] We have felt "something is missing" for awhile but we rationalize and try to be comfortable with things the way they are. We keep each other at arm's length.

[ ] We stay busy or have some compulsive issues that keep us from even wanting to get too close. We feel emotionally distant until one of us pulls away, gets mad, or is moody. Things change a little, then go right back to the way they were.

Acting Out Issues

[ ] One or both of us has a lot of triggered feelings (anger, anxiety, pain, depression) that keep our relationship in drama too often.

[ ] We aren't a team on many important things. We have some power-struggles, arguments, blame each other, feel upset a lot.

[ ] We feel very attached to each other but we fight. One of us feels he/she does too much, gives too much, puts up with too much.

[ ] We have poor boundaries with each other and one/both of us feels emotionally taken for granted or even abused.

[ ] We blame each other and both of us have our "walls". We don't see our own part or any way to make it better. We feel stuck.

[ ] We threaten to leave and then have "talks", promises, even good behavior, and make-up sex. It only lasts until we get close again.

Name_____   Date_____

How do you handle your Needs & Feelings?

Are you open & emotionally available enough for a higher level of love?

[　]I tend to think I don't need very much, am self-sufficient, don't open up, I stay "ON", "UP", "FINE" most of the time

[　]I tend to be "in my head" too much, I analyze, plan, think, and rationalize my feelings, tend to deny, avoid problems

[　]I feel sort of flat, blah, tired, or stressed/overwhelmed a lot and don't "date", have fun, or bring energy to the relationship

[　]I have some physical problems associated with buried, repressed feelings: headaches, insomnia, stomach problems

[　]I am edgy, angry, moody a lot and sometimes it comes out at my partner, or just gets bottled up inside and I withdraw

[　]I feel like I can't really let go and just relax without feeling like I "have to do something productive", to stay busy, am wound up

[　]I have a problem with addictions and/or compulsive issues: work, TV, games/porn/chat rooms, addictive sex, spending, other

[　]I am not in recovery or therapy for my addictions or compulsive problems, mood problems; I expect my partner to put up with it

[　]Sometimes I think I am too needy, that I never "get enough" and feel empty inside, or demand a lot from my partner

[　]I notice my feelings when I am upset, in a crisis, or when they are very intense, but not on a regular/everyday, routine basis

[　]I keep my guard up so no one really "gets in", I am strong

[　]I give a lot, do for others, but don't focus on my own self, my focus is on taking care of others, I stay in control, am closed

[　]I scold myself, preach to myself, tell myself "stiff upper lip", and generally talk myself out of feelings and needs, rationalize

[　]I have trouble just being alone, I feel "anzty", bored, or can't relax when I'm alone, I don't like to be alone

[　]My partner has to "pull teeth" to get me to talk about feelings and then I give one word answers, I am always in control

[　]I know what I feel but I don't open up, can't seem to find the words to communicate in a way so issues get resolved, I stay closed

[　]I express most needs in a one-dimensional way, I just want a "fix" for sex, a drug, or an escape, I expect nurturing without depth

Name_____ Date_____

Can you manage your Moods & Feelings?

Are you an emotional burden on love?
Are core wounds with buried feelings a problem?

[ ] My anger really gets out of control!

[ ] I get triggered over everyday things.

[ ] I vent my anger at my partner too often!

[ ] Save me! My life is a mess! I'm stuck!

[ ] I need someone! I'm not independent!

[ ] I don't have goals, a plan, or a real focus!

[ ] I get overwhelmed, freaked out, and upset !

[ ] I get really anxious, stressed too often!

[ ] Life is hard, a struggle, and I can't win!

[ ] I have depression and pain, feel down a lot.

[ ] I don't have much energy for fun or dates.

[ ] I need my partner to "be there" for me.

[ ] I can't slow down! I always do too much!

[ ] I live "in my head", with my "to do" list.

[ ] I overdo, I feel stressed, I can't say "no"!

I'm tired of your anger and nagging! Stop trying to control me!

You have to change too! I give too much! I just do it all!

THESE PATTERNS BUILD "WALLS"!
These patterns keep relationships stuck, angry and distant!

- **BLAMING** keeps us stuck, angry and adversaries
  This is caused by victim-martyr patterns, and you need to learn how to voice feelings, be "heard" instead of silent resentment!

- **BUILDING A CASE** is "being right", not being a team
  Even if you're right, building your case isn't being open and hearing your partner's point of view. It's a bit controlling, and too one-sided. You have 50% of the responsibility!

- **BEING INNOCENT** being righteous and confused
  Staying unaware, innocent, righteous and confused means that you aren't owning your 50% of the responsibility for issues.

- **MAKING EXCUSES** being dependent, passive and stuck
  Not working at making this relationship healthier and growing out of your patterns (not putting in effort) is a dependent way to avoid changes and it sabotages being close in mature ways.

- **BOUNDARY ISSUES** personal power, having a voice
  Codependency issues and unhealthy childhood dependency keep you stuck without boundaries, not expecting enough mature behavior from your partner. This is enabling and isn't healthy.

- **ACTING OUT BURIED FEELINGS** triggered anger
  Triggered anger, negative moods, complaining and blaming are acted out in relationships and become a burden on any partner.

- **SEXUAL DEMANDS** "guilt or needy" sex isn't reciprocal
  Sex without real connection is often due to pressure, guilt, or using sex as a substitute for a lack of closeness when couples are stuck in their patterns.

REPROGRAMMING TOOLS:
WORKING WITH OUR PATTERNS

What causes our walls? Describe a problem in our relationship that causes a silent wall of resentment. What are some of the patterns that push me away, cause me to shut down, feel distant, or lose desire...

Do these common patterns cause a "wall"?

- **Blaming, pointing the finger , holding on to a list of resentments without taking some of the responsibility for why we feel stuck**

- **Building a case, making my partner wrong, trying to be right, often feeling "innocent", like a victim or a martyr, or "righteous"**

- **Being "innocent", staying unaware of my own part (my 50%) in our dynamics, feeling like a helpless child with my partner**

- **I use excuses to stay the same, to keep having my partner take care of me, I feel entitled to be demanding and non-reciprocal**

- **Boundary issues, codependency and unhealthy dependency keep us both stuck, resentful, and we both feel controlled somewhat**

- **Sexual demands, pressure, needy sex, sex as a fix without mature closeness, a lack of real connection, warmth, romance, energy**

- **Unhealthy lifestyle issues (drinking, drugs, compulsive habits, being too busy or being a workaholic) keep us angry and in drama**

Name_____ **Date**_____

We want to take down our "walls"!

Journal about something you are having a problem feeling "heard" about, that you haven't felt you can really communicate openly about.

Journal about something your partner does that pushes you away and how you react and handle it when it happens.

Journal about a feeling you have when your partner is being needy and a little demanding. How do you react and handle it?

Name_____ Date_____

Journal about something you or your partner "points the finger" about, blames, complains and doesn't offer real support and help about.

Journal about a recent conversation that left you both frustrated, at odds, and feeling discouraged about. What makes this hard?

Journal about a feeling you have when your partner is moody. How does this affect you? Do your partner's moods control you?

Take turns and practice talking for 10 minutes about these issues.

[   ] I initiated journaling-talking as a team: _____.

[   ] My partner initiated journaling-talking as a team: _____.

Name_____ Date_____

GROWING OUR RELATIONSHIP TOGETHER

HEART-CENTERED LOVE

PROGRAMMING
stuck in unhealthy
patterns

REPROGRAMMING
a higher level of
love

Our Level of Emotional Trust

Week 4	Reprogramming Tools Exercises, Homework and Tools
Our Level of Emotional Trust	• **Emotional trust effects passion, desire** • **Communication increases trust** • **What we want to improve in our relationship** • **Do we have low levels of emotional trust?** • **Problems with reciprocal nourishment**

EMOTIONAL TRUST

Emotional trust is the feeling you have when you know you can go to someone and they will **"be there"** for you. You can go to this person with your feelings and you can depend on this partner to show caring, to give you emotional support, to be nourishing. It is not the same thing as having someone just "fix it" for you, give you a solution or tell you what you should do. In fact this often feels critical or unnourishing. When emotional trust is at a high level we feel **close, warm, we feel loving**. Emotional trust increases desire and attraction. It is a **key to a healthy, passionate sex life**. There are several important areas of confusion about emotional trust that keep couples stuck.

One area of confusion is the **difference between being needy** and real emotional trust, where you feel nourishing to your partner. Emotional trust will not be high, you **won't feel nourishing** to your partner, sex and romance won't improve, if you're really going through the motions and **being needy and demanding**. Your partner may have some dependency issues and tolerate this but emotional trust won't be high. This is because you are approaching your partner from the **wounded, immature, needy part** of your personality. This never feels good and certainly isn't about "being there" for your partner. To feel nourishing to your partner you have to learn how to bring the most mature, highest-functioning part of your personality to your relationship. This is the only part of you with **something to give.** You can use tools to learn how to shift out of the wounded, immature, needy part of yourself. When you do this routinely, emotional trust will improve. The wounded part of you always feels like **a burden on a partner**. It's too moody, too negative, too angry, too needy, and filled with buried feelings. It's **not love's job** to fix this. You need to do this internally, to bring some of your positive and healthy energy to your partner. Then you aren't being dependent and enemshed.

Another area of confusion about emotional trust is the **feeling of entitlement**. Children are entitled to yell, scream, whine, moan and groan every feeling they impulsively have and act out all their moods. Adults aren't entitled to do this and they are being **emotionally demanding and immature** when they do. Your negative feelings and moods are **your own responsibility**. Acting them out by feeling stuck in them, leaving your partner no option but to tolerate them, isn't nourishing and your partner will withdraw from you. Emotional trust will be very low and neither of you will feel nourished or close. No one wants to be a 24-7 therapist, parent, or shoulder for another adult's most wounded, most triggered, most immature, negative moods. This isn't what intimacy and love is supposed to provide for adults. Emotional trust is high when **support is reciprocal.**

RE-BUILD EMOTIONAL TRUST TOGETHER

Emotional Trust affects Passion, Sex, and Closeness!

Increase emotional trust with your partner!

1. Do you **trust your partner** to listen and show concern for your feelings? Does your partner ask questions about why you feel the way you do? Do you show your partner the same concern?

2. Do you **trust your partner** to give you emotional support when you are hurting instead of being defensive or shutting you out, ignoring what you feel and need?

3. Do you **expect your partner** to say "I'm sorry" or "I made a mistake" or even "I was wrong" once in a while? Do you also do this?

4. Can you really bring up heartfelt issues and problems and **"feel heard"** by your partner? Does your partner feel heard by you?

5. Do you feel your partner sees your good points, strengths, and best qualities and is **nourishing** about them? Are you? Or do you feel criticized and examined through a negative lens by your partner?

6. Does your partner **appreciate** what you bring to the relationship and tell you it is appreciated? Is it good enough? Do you feel appreciated or taken for granted, used, needed but not really loved?

7. Does your partner **put forth an effort** to do what it takes to be healthy enough to have a quality relationship or just blame you, expect you to **accept, enable, settle** for very little adult behavior? Or for a limited sexual relationship?

8. Does your partner feel **inviting emotionally and open to a real connection** with you? Do you feel warm, have fun, flirt and play before having sex? Do you have **quality romance** and make it a priority? Does your partner initiate this?

9. Do you expect **understanding, support, and appreciation** from your partner? Do you give it to your partner on a regular basis? Do you both feel nourished and feel like "we are on the **same team**"!

Open up about ISSUES, PROBLEMS, FEELINGS

· "I notice we are being fine, *like roommates again*. I'm glad we aren't fighting but I want us to be able to *really talk, to open up to each other*. I want to bring up some feelings I'm writing about, some resentments I carry around in my head." (it takes two to stay distant)

· "I want to bring up some of my resentments but I know you have some also. Let's get these feelings out in the open so we can work on it together. We both seem to be *stuck holding onto a lot of anger, blame*." (you both have to get your old baggage and resentments out of the way)

· "How could I approach you differently that would not push you away? I really do want to change. I am beginning to see how I *blame you and stay adversarial*." (adversarial means you don't notice the partner's needs/feelings, try to prove they are wrong, argue but don't listen to the feelings behind the words, end the communication, don't work as a team)

· "We are both angry and so invested in being right, we aren't talking about how our real feelings (lonely, hurt, empty, boring, painful, sad, scary) caused by the distance, by not feeling enough emotional trust. I feel a lot of feelings *besides my anger*. I want to discuss these feelings."

· "I notice you are *withdrawing and being alone, staying distant from me* (avoiding sex, or staying gone, etc.). Would you try to talk about why? I'd really like to know." (bringing up the distance)

· "I don't feel *nourished emotionally* anymore. I wonder if you feel nourished by me emotionally? We don't seem to trust each other to "be there" emotionally for each other. I don't feel my feelings are taken seriously. (asking for more involvement)

What works!
YOUR "ADULT VOICE" IS A TOOL!
Using the ADULT VOICE
increases EMOTIONAL TRUST!

Increasing Emotional Trust in COMMUNICATION

Oops! Problems ahead!

- Do you "end" the conversation?
- Do you talk "at" not "with" your partner?
- Do you get triggered and it escalates?
- Do you invite feedback? Are you open?
- Is it "all about your feelings"?
- Do you stay adversarial? Do you vent?

Listening and Being Heard

- Show interest, make eye contact, lean forward
- Reflect back what is said, show some interest, caring
- Ask questions, draw out the feelings of your partner
- It's not about agreeing, it's about really "hearing"
- Don't let the content distract you, hear the needs and feelings and your partner's point of view

A FEW COMMUNICATION PROBLEMS

[   ]interrupting, rolling eyes, sarcasm, poor attention, not listening

[   ]changing the subject, being dramatic, over-reacting, exaggerating

[   ]me, me, me! changing the focus back to your feelings

[   ]building a case, defending, holding onto grudges, staying angry

[   ]stopping the flow so nothing gets resolved, bouncing around

[   ]arguing, bickering, picky at details to avoid a real solution

[   ]making your partner wrong, "being right" and righteous

[   ]threats, ultimatums, leaving the room, using threats to
     end the relationship or withdraw (I'm leaving, I give up!)

[   ]"if you loved me", you would do it my way, being controlling

[   ]"you owe me", using guilt and obligation to get needs met

[   ]being right, being self-righteous, "innocent", unaware

[   ]feeling controlled by your partner is a communication pattern
     that keeps you stuck (even if your partner is controlling)

[   ]lack of empathy for your partner's feelings is a problem

[   ]steam-rolling, being a bully, getting into a threatening posture

[   ]being impatient, dismissive, acting bored, being critical, superior

Name_____   Date_____

● **Ask for what you want ahead of time, especially when you have been disappointed in the past. Don't set up another disappointment.**
"Honey I notice that you're usually an hour late for dinner. I'll cook but would you change the time or arrive when I get it on the table? If you don't want this pressure today just get your own meal and I won't prepare a meal? What would you like to do?" ... **setting a boundary/communicating directly**

● **Stop blaming your partner (by being right, building a case, holding a grudge, staying in your head). Invite solutions by owning your issues, taking healthy responsibility, and being part of the solution. Staying stuck is lonely!**
"I know I was irritable and tense and snapped at you. I would not like it if you snapped at me that way. I guess I react to you with anger too often. In my head I make you wrong. I'm really going to start working on making some changes in how I tend to approach you. I'm not inviting you to be close to me, am I?"...**owns some of the responsibility, is becoming more aware of patterns, opens the communication in an inviting way**

● **Avoid having the relationship "in your head". This causes distance and is not intimate or nourishing.**
"I'm mad because I just assume you are pushing me away, being cold toward me. I tend to give you the silent treatment right back. I guess this is not being intimate. I wonder if you're feeling distant with me right now? Would you discuss it with me?" ...**asking direct questions and being more open in the communication/removing the wall**

● **Demands and ultimatums (I want what I want right now, my way, or you don't love me) don't work. It is not your partner's job to satisfy every emotional need, soothe all of your feelings, take care of your intense emotional reactions and moods. Nor is it yours!**
"Your anger is sharp and biting. I don't want to get pulled into a fight because you feel irritable. I'm sorry but we can discuss this issue or problem without this much anger. You are dumping on me. And you're not handling your moods and feelings. I'm not 'the dump' for your bottled up anger!"...**not participating in drama, setting healthy limits, expecting reasonable mature behavior**

♥ I CAN ONLY CHANGE MYSELF!
I CAN CHOOSE TO REACT IN HEALTHIER WAYS INSTEAD OF BEING PART OF THE PROBLEM!

CHANGES TO IMPROVE OUR EMOTIONAL TRUST

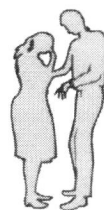

- Become **more of a team**-not adversaries with power-struggles
- Each take our own **50% of responsibility for problems**
- **Initiate changes**-ask to talk, journal, use tools together
- **Move out of blaming**, complaints without real boundaries, being a victim, feeling used, staying angry and venting
- **Expect more** mature, healthy behavior from each other, approach each other with energy, be more nourishing
- Learn realistic expectations, and **practice healthy boundaries**

WHAT WE WANT TO IMPROVE

[　] COMMUNICATION-not feeling heard, it escalates or ends

[　] SHARING RESPONSIBILITES-lack of partnership and support

[　] NURTURING EACH OTHER EMOTIONALLY-issues of
affection, warmth, mature closeness, empathy

[　] SEXUAL DISTANCE-sex without passion, dates without
connection, attraction, desire, openness, as a "fix"

[　] NOT DATING WITH ENERGY-not bringing a mature
feeling and energy to dates, dates aren't enough fun

[　] MONEY ISSUES-not being a team, a couple with money

[　] EMOTIONAL TRUST-abuse, criticism, insults, jabs, "teasing"

[　] BOUNDARY ISSUES-excuses, tolerating immature or
unhealthy behavior, controlling, passive-aggressive

[　] MOODS ARE A BURDEN-one partner has too many
negative moods, is moody, negative, "heavy" a lot

[　] DEPENDENCY WITH OTHERS THAT IS A WEDGE-too
much family, a child, friends, or emotional infidelity

[　] ADDICTIONS-COMPULSIVE PROBLEMS-problems with
addictions, compulsive habits keep us in turmoil

Name_____ Date_____

Communication with a FOCUS!
Couples who journal learn how to focus and communication improves!

JOURNAL ABOUT OUR EMOTIONAL TRUST

Learning how to open up and talk about emotional trust is the first step in describing what you both need. BE SPECIFIC-the more specific you are, the better your communication will be! Getting ready with journaling before you talk together helps you have more clear, focused communication.

Isn't love worth it!

Our emotional trust is low and we aren't close, warm, and nourishing enough to each other. What keeps us stuck or distant? Do we feel deprived emotionally? BE SPECIFIC.

What I would really like for my partner TO DO TO MAKE CHANGES in this area? To feel more nourishing and to be more reciprocal so we both feel like "lovers" again.

NOW TALK IT OVER TOGETHER!

Write about how your communication about emotional trust felt this time. Remember growth isn't magic. Be patient and it will improve gradually!

Name_____   Date_____

EMOTIONAL TRUST
THE FOUNDATION FOR
A HIGHER LEVEL OF LOVE

Couples who are distant emotionally, stay frustrated, angry, moody, and feel like they have to stay on the surface to get along ("roommates") don't have high levels of EMOTIONAL TRUST. It is important to increase the level of emotional trust in your relationship in order for both partners to feel nourished. UNHEALTHY DEPENDENCY CAUSES EMOTIONAL TRUST to be low. Unhealthy dependency is not reciprocal nourishment or healthy!

Do we have LOW LEVELS OF EMOTIONAL TRUST?

[   ] I don't feel my partner is "there" for me emotionally. Most of the time in our relationship I listen and am there for my partner but it isn't reciprocal.

[   ] I can't lean on my partner for support, reassurance, to feel cared for, to have appropriate attention, to feel nourished. My partner is shut down.

[   ] One of us is moody, irritated, angry, negative, or tired or stressed out a lot. We don't have enough quality fun together! We don't play!

[   ] My partner makes excuses and ignores my needs. It's a one-sided relationship. My partner is acts innocent and is closed! I feel controlled.

[   ] I ask for reasonable, healthy nourishment, romance, connection but my partner won't meet me half-way. I have to "push, beg, prod" often.

[   ] We both stay distracted, "on the surface" until someone gets moody, acts out anger. We can't talk openly and feel stuck "on the surface".

[   ] We don't go on "dates" and have special time for us as a couple that makes us feel closer, romantic, sexual. We aren't "lovers" and don't date.

[   ] Our dates aren't intimate, close, or much romantic fun. We stay at arm's length. We don't flirt and play anymore. We don't date as "lovers".

Name_____ Date_____

RECIPROCAL NOURISHMENT

When support and nourishment is two-sided and reciprocal emotional trust improves. One-sided, needy, immature demands for support, reassurance and attention keep emotional trust low! Negative moods are a burden! Being moody often is unhealthy dependency.

PROBLEMS WITH RECIPROCAL NOURISHMENT
circle the problems below you're each having now

- A partner expects sex without connection, closeness, flirting, affection

- A partner doesn't bring healthy moods, energy, being fun on dates

- A partner feels entitled to "act out" negative moods, vent, blame

- A partner is tired, sick, stressed, too busy, has lots of excuses

- A partner can't talk without it escalating, "blaming", acting out

- A partner doesn't show enough warmth, caring, nurturing

- A partner needs too much attention for moods, negative emotions

- A partner keeps the other "at arm's length", won't try to be close

YOUR PARTNER FELL IN LOVE WITH THE HIGHEST-FUNCTIONING, MOST MATURE, ATTRACTIVE, AND HEALTHY PART OF YOU...
Not your "emotional baggage"!

Childhood dependency is a one-way kind of dependency (children need it and thrive on it) we learn from our families in childhood. Healthy, nourishing adult relationships are supposed to be more **reciprocal and to nourish both of the partners.** Unhealthy dependency from childhood is not reciprocal or mature! The most wounded part of each partner feels entitled to "act out" and be taken care of emotionally, to lean on the relationship, to be a burden with negative moods. This causes sexual issues, communication problems and low levels of emotional trust.

GROWING OUR RELATIONSHIP TOGETHER

HEART-CENTERED LOVE

PROGRAMMING
stuck in unhealthy
patterns

REPROGRAMMING
a higher level of
love

Giving and Receiving Feedback

Week 5	Reprogramming Tools Exercises, Homework and Tools
Giving- Receiving Feedback	• Are you "in your head"-not in your heart? • Feedback deepens our communication • Do we "act out" anger too much? • Money, Chores, Sex: giving-receiving feedback • Talking homework-Feedback • Dating like "lovers" again

COMMUNICATION AND FEEDBACK

Open communication involves **giving each other feedback** about how we feel, what we need, what isn't working and what feels good, what our strengths are. Some partners **deflect honest feedback** by doing things that end communication. This is unhealthy because the problems fester and become worse over time instead of getting resolved. Sometimes partners don't tolerate much feedback because it's done in an abusive style instead of a sharing style. When you each learn how to **take 50 % of the responsibility** for the issue you are discussing, it works wonders and makes the other partner want to listen more. After all no one wants to just get a bunch of non-productive anger dumped on them. This isn't feedback and it's counterproductive. Feedback is actually **very productive** and opens up communication channels. When you can't give feedback to each other the communication is being controlled by some unhealthy patterns and you may need a therapist to help open it up.

Sometimes partners are stuck, living and feeling **"in their head" too much** and can't be open emotionally. That's because they aren't connected to their authentic reactions and feelings, probably don't know how to be present, gloss things over, stay detached and only share when having **a meltdown**. If this is you, it will keep your relationship stuck unless you use some tools to **focus, be specific, stop rationalizing and discounting** your feelings. You will tend to blame your feelings on your partner if you aren't getting your needs met, but lack the mature boundaries in a more vibrant love. **Journaling is a process** to help you get "out of your head" and become more connected to yourself, your feelings and your needs.

Money and sex are two important aspects of adult life that really reveal relationship dynamics. If you aren't **a couple with money** you probably aren't a team in your relationship. If you **feel controlled and don't take adult responsibility** for decision-making you may be taking an immature position with your partner. This will show up in other ways too. Talk together about both of you being adults, working together **as a team**, being a couple with money.

No one signs up for marriage and love without sex. You both expect fidelity from each other and have made a **commitment to provide the sexual part** of your relationship to each other. The problem is sex is fragile and desire and attraction diminish when a relationship isn't nourishing. Giving and asking for feedback is important in finding out how you can **become a more nourishing partner. Dating as lovers,** (not as friends to get out of the house) is a step to a more nourishing, mature relationship. Bring some **energy and be a fun companion!**

Are you "in your head" too much?
(and not "in your heart"!)

I IGNORE MYSELF and STAY DETACHED what needs & feelings?

"I don't have time!"

" I stay distracted, busy, unaware of my needs and feelings, I don't pay much attention to my needs, feelings...
I DON'T EVEN RECOGNIZE WHAT THEY ARE..."

[ ]I give to others (codependency) to feel needed, I'm "last"
[ ]I deny, minimize, avoid, stuff, or rationalize my feelings away
[ ]I only notice feelings when they get very intense, needy
[ ]I often feel blah, flat, tired, or stressed when I'm not "doing"
[ ]I don't feel nourished, rarely feel full, "run on empty", don't think about how I feel, what my life is like, just stay busy

I BEAT MYSELF UP Constant criticism & pressure

"I should have done it better!"

" I beat myself up inside, I'm self-critical, and view myself with a negative lens, I feel I'm never quite good enough,
I SHOULD ALWAYS BE BETTER & DO MORE..."

[ ]I push, pressure myself to be better, be more perfect, have a lot of "SHOULDS" (should look diff, should be a certain way, should do more, etc.)
[ ]I often think of my flaws, things I haven't done, "failings", mistakes
[ ]I compare myself to others often and feel "less than"
[ ]I allow others to criticize, demean me, be rude, even insult me
[ ]I am very critical of myself, never feel I'm "good enough"

I LECTURE MYSELF I give myself pep talks

"Get over it! It's no big deal!"

" I lecture myself inside, give myself pep talks, tell myself to be better, try harder, I talk myself out of my feelings,
I RATIONALIZE MY FEELINGS AWAY..."

[ ] When I feel insecure, when I need support, I tell myself to get over it
[ ]I pressure myself to be "up" most of the time, not to feel or need much
[ ]I don't give myself much support, nurturing, attention, pampering
[ ]I rationalize my feelings, stuff them down, ignore my feelings, they'll pass!
[ ]I feel I am "weak" if I'm not in control, staying busy, being productive

What does this have to do with my relationship problems?

Being "in your head" interferes with communication being deep enough to make a real connection. Instead it stays superficial which isn't nourishing and keeps both partners feeling somewhat "alone", one the surface, and partners often feel controlled.

What's the big deal? So I'm "in my head"!

We don't feel like "lovers"

- We have sexual issues, loss of desire and attraction
- We can't talk without it escalating into a fight
- We don't flirt with each other and play together
- Everything is serious or a heavy "talk" about problems
- Our dates feel dry and stale, even a little boring
- We aren't connected emotionally unless it's drama
- The only time we talk is when one of us is mad, moody

SYMPTOMS OF BEING DETACHED ("in my head")

[　] I "gloss over " things over and overlook the real problems, what I feel

[　] I "talk myself out of it" often and I ignore my feelings in the moment

[　] I focus on what my partner feels and needs, on his/her moods usually

[　] I "take care of myself" and try not to need much, don't lean, stay busy

[　] I'm with a partner who is moody often and needs my support often

[　] I make excuses for my partner and tolerate immature, selfish behavior

[　] I deny my deeper feelings and my needs and just stay in control

[　] I avoid too much closeness, I withdraw from it usually, it feels needy

[　] When I am not detached, busy or stressed, I start to feel uneasy, bored

[　] I keep everyone at arm's length and "take care of" what others need

[　] I "go through the motions" sexually , try to keep my partner satisfied

[　] I don't really want to be too close, because my partner is mad a lot

[　] I don't get much emotional nourishment but I'm ok without it

[　] We talk about feelings too much, it's always a heavy "talk"

Name_____   **Date**_____

MY INNER RELATIONSHIP
"living in your head" causes relationship problems
How I treat myself is mirrored in my outer relationships

The way our emotional world feels actually makes some sense when you look at what it's a reflection of. For example if people close to you tend to ignore your needs or only think of themselves, it is likely this could not go on unless you were also detached, ignoring your needs, unaware of what it would even look like to feel different. If you are with a woman who is demanding, Mom or Dad probably was, and you may automatically tend to please, give in, deny what you need but need a lot of attention for negative moods. If you're with a man who is a bully with his moods, maybe a parent was scary and you learned to pamper this kind of self-absorbed, demanding behavior by denying your feelings and talking yourself out of them, thinking you don't deserve respect and calm. How do you treat your needs, feelings?

[　] I am too critical of myself　　I mentally compare myself to others

I judge myself often　　I have to be perfect, feel a lot of pressure

I feel either superior or inferior　　I am very competitive, have to win

I don't like myself much　　I am hard on others and on myself

I analyze, worry, overthink small things　　I get angry and blow up

I was criticized, pressured, or molded too much in my childhood

[　] I can't slow down, plan too much　　I feel empty when I'm alone

I have few close friends　　I am controlling, sometimes even rigid

I have buried anger/angry moods　　I don't know my needs, feelings

I feel tired, bored or zoned out a lot　　I can't say no without guilt

I give/do too much, want to be needed　　I have poor boundaries

I let people use me, walk on me　　I say "yes" to be liked

I was smothered, controlled or neglected, abused in my childhood

[　] I don't expect much nourishment, support or notice it's not there

I tolerate abuse, make excuses　I talk myself out of my feelings

No one gets too close to me, "gets in"　　I have no real joy inside

I am anxious a lot but don't show it　　I have no passion in my life

I accept crumbs in relationships　　I get moody in a vague way

My life feels like a treadmill　　I am guarded, closed, "fine", "up", "on"

I was neglected, ignored or abused in my childhood

Name_____ Date_____

TALKING IS NOT VENTING!

COMMUNICATION
IS NOT "ACTING OUT" MOODS
GETTING and GIVING FEEDBACK!

[   ] My partner wants me to stop being mad, edgy, or venting instead of discussing issues and feelings in reasonable ways.

[   ] My partner wants me to be more open and emotionally available, not just staying on the surface about our problems and issues.

[   ] My partner wants me to be less controlling and demanding with my moods and feelings and change the way I handle some of my reactions.

[   ] My partner wants me to stop "going through the motions", staying on the surface, and then complaining about it later.

[   ] My partner wants me to be more mature and healthy in our sex life: bring mature energy, be fun and sexy, flirt, plan and initiate. Do my part!

[   ] My partner says I don't invite, attract, act playful, flirtatious enough on our dates, bring enough romance, and sensuality to our relationship.

[   ] My partner wants me to put more effort and commitment in our couples work so we grow out of being stuck (talk more, use tools, journal, do the exercises together).   This is our means to an end!

[   ] My partner feels I stay distant, on the surface, but then expect to be taken care of and nourished without much real mature closeness.

[   ] My partner wants affection to be reciprocal (two way, not one-way), and to have more connection, support, understanding, and deeper talking.

[   ] My partner thinks I "have to be right" instead of looking at my 50% of the responsibility for why we aren't close and playful much anymore.

[   ] My partner says I don't accept feedback without becoming angry and moody, that I need to start to make changes, not promise to change!

NAME _____ **DATE**_____

**I have to
do some stuff!**

**I'm just too
stressed!**

We stay on the surface!
We are detached!

- When we talk about feelings it's because one of us gets mad or is moody!

- When we talk about feelings, it's the "heavy" stuff! It's a downer!

- When we talk about feelings, it's because one of us feels triggered!

- We are "in our head" when we try to talk! We don't get problems resolved.

- We stay on the surface most of the time. We know there is some tension but we don't bring things up. We are used to a "wall" and don't talk, just "let it slide". If we talk it doesn't resolve the issue anyway.

- We both live in our separate worlds most of the time. We don't really feel close. I usually talk myself out of my feelings. I keep everything inside. This makes me stuff a lot of feelings but at least we get along.

- Something really "bad" has to happen before we admit there is a problem. We tend to live "on the surface", are "fine" usually. I am used to this and don't want to have to dig up feelings and open up.

Describe three things I don't usually bring up...that I keep silent about or just put up with and tend to ignore, tolerate, or rationalize to myself.

1.

2.

3.

Name_____   Date_____

Do we act out our "baggage"?
A checklist for signs of
CONTROL ISSUES
BURIED ANGER
PASSIVE-AGGRESSIVE ANGER

BURIED ANGER causes distance (WALLS) in all intimate relationships. Anger and abusive patterns are usually repeated from one relationship to the next, often with very little awareness. Being shut down is an angry pattern. Partners with angry patterns are often unaware that they relate in these patterns. Sometimes anger is expressed as passive-aggressive (distant) patterns. Intimacy cannot grow and mature when anger is a wall between partners.

DO WE HAVE SOME UNRESOLVED ANGER?

[ ] **We bicker about small, everyday things, then stuff it.**

[ ] **One of us threatens to end the relationship too often, has one foot out the door, or just leaves "inside" by fantasizing about leaving.**

[ ] **One or both partners tend to blame the other for many relationship problems, without trying to accept his/her half (50%) of the issues and take some responsibility. Stalemate.**

[ ] **Communication ends quickly without anyone being "heard". Problems are ignored not resolved. We get along on the surface.**

[ ] **One partner controls the relationship by threatening to leave, get needs met elsewhere, rather than solve issues.**

[ ] **One or both partners is addictive with drugs, alcohol, work, or sex and is too compulsive to be intimate in healthy ways.**

[ ] **One partner "steamrolls" the other into verbal submission, giving in, giving up.**

[ ] **Name-calling, blaming, attacking, venting, and accusing is abuse.**

[ ] **One or both partners are angry, moody, irritated often and take it out on the relationship, lean on the relationship too much.**

[ ] **There is unresolved anger underneath a superficial layer of control, a making "nice" layer, and the anger gets triggered regularly.**

[ ] **One partner tells the other that the anger, problems are his/her fault, that he/she over-reacts, one partner "makes the other partner wrong".**

[ ] **One partner denies, minimizes, avoids the issues, stays superficial.**

Name-_____ Date-_____

- **MY GROWTH DOES NOT DEPEND ON MY PARTNER.**

It is natural to have moods, disappointments, frustrations, and resentments in all relationships. I can choose healthy ways or unhealthy ways to handle my emotional reactions, expectations, feelings, issues and our problems.

- **MY EMOTIONAL REACTIONS ARE NOT CAUSED BY MY PARTNER. MY REACTIONS ARE MY OWN RESPONSIBILITY!**

My partner may be difficult, abusive, or immature, but I can react in healthy ways and communicate openly, set limits, and learn to avoid over-reacting while I learn how to grow into having better boundaries.

- **I CAN LEARN TOOLS TO REACT BY COMMUNICATING WITH HEALTHY BOUNDARIES and HEALTHY DEPENDENCY.**

How I react depends on how I accept my personal (50%)responsibility for my moods and feelings, how I choose to handle our issues, and how I set boundaries, communicate, and practice healthy dependency. "How could I be more open, receptive, intimate and mature in how I choose to deal with our issues and react to them or handle problems?"

THESE PATTERNS KEEP OUR RELATIONSHIP STUCK!

[　]blaming, "making your partner wrong", having to be right

[　]withdrawing from each other, punishing when it isn't my way

[　]accusing, attacking, venting, exploding, steamrolling, "bullying"

[　]lecturing, rambling, being a "know it all", talking "at not with"

[　]acting superior, being righteous, smug or condescending

[　]changing the subject, interrupting, not sharing the talking

[　]nit-picking, focusing on minor details, avoiding real changes

[　]staying "innocent", confused, denying your issues, unaware

[　]building a case, finding reasons to stay angry, justifying anger

[　]my way or the highway, being rigid, closed, controlling

[　]threats to leave, to cheat, to get a divorce, be destructive

[　]"if you loved me", you would do it how I want, guilt trips

[　]keeping my partner "on edge" with negative moods, anger

[　]one of us is too wound up to relax and just "let go", to "be there"

Name_____ **Date**_____

FFEEDBACK about OUR RESPONSIBILITES and FINANCES

RESPONSIBILITES AND FINANCES   (HINT: discuss this together)

*directions: cross out the part that doesn't fit-all parts of a point may not fit for you

[   ]We do not share our chores in a flowing adult way, one is "the boss", the other is like "the kid" who has to be reminded and prodded usually

[   ]We do not have a plan for sharing finances that empowers us as a couple, one partner runs the show, makes the decisions, controls the purse-strings

[   ]We argue about money, we aren't a team, we don't feel like a couple about money

[   ]We have too much clutter, mess, don't work together to make a comfortable space

[   ]One partner does most of the "work", feels burdened, complains, or resents it

[   ]My partner will help out only if I tell him/her what to do each time, I have to nag

[   ]My partner complains about our finances but spends too much, doesn't work with me to budget, just spends when he/she wants to

[   ]We aren't a couple with financial goals and working toward some financial dreams

[   ]I am financially dependent on my partner who provides all the expenses and treats me like a child on an allowance, I feel controlled instead of like an adult

[   ]Even though we are married, it is still "his" or "her" money, we have separate finances and we feel like we are very separate

[   ]We do not have a joint account together, with separate spending money for each of us so we aren't in a position of asking for spending money

[   ]I feel like a child, I have to ask for cash when I need it or get permission

[   ]My partner takes care of the finances, handles that stuff, I don't even know how much we have , and really don't want to be bothered

[   ]We spend too much for our income, we don't work on living within our means, we can't budget, we don't sit down and work as a team together

[   ]We don't have any financial goals as a couple, don't make plans as a couple

[   ]Finances are the main reason I stay in this relationship because I am not very fulfilled in it in most other important ways, I am not fulfilled as a man or woman

[   ]I do too much of the chores and don't feel appreciated, feel taken for granted, even "used" in some ways, we both work full time and aren't a balanced team

[   ]My partner does not pull his /her "weight" around the house so I take over and do it all, my partner does things in a half-baked way to sabotage really doing it

[   ]I bitch, nag, complain, even threaten but nothing changes and I have to pick up after my partner who is messy/cluttered/ leaves junk around, expects me to pick up

[   ]My partner makes big/important financial decisions without me, I have no real voice, power or I just go along and am not part of the decision-making

[   ]I resent our financial arrangement and don't feel empowered in it

[   ]I resent the way we share our responsibilities and don't feel "heard" about it

Journal about our FINANCES & SHARED RESPONSIBILITIES ISSUES

Name_____ Date_____

FEEDBACK about ROMANCE and SEXUALITY

ROMANCE and SEXUALITY **(HINT: discuss this together)**

*directions: cross out the part that doesn't fit-all parts of a point may not fit for you

[   ]We are not romantic, don't make any time for "dates" together, are comfortable "best friends" but "something is missing", sometimes it is boring

[   ]Sex feels like a chore to one or both of us, is too mechanical, lacks passion, real playfulness, we don't flirt or show interest in each other

[   ]There are other problems that effect our sex life: depression, resentments, lack of closeness, frequent fights, addictions, or too much distance between us

[   ]My partner does not seem to want to improve our sex life, won't admit there is a problem, avoids the subject, has excuses, doesn't try to be my "lover"

[   ]My partner is withholding sexually, tends to refuse to have sex or show not much real interest (unless we fight, I give him/ her an ultimatum)

[   ]My partner has a "sexual demand" for sex , expects me to have sex often or gets moody, threatens to cheat on me, gets mad, needs sex to feel ok

[   ]I feel a somewhat constant pressure to meet my partner's needs, my own needs get pushed aside and ignored, my partner makes me responsible for making it work and for why we aren't passionate

[   ]We don't really have much fun together: we are always working, stressed about something, are too busy, don't have time or energy for fun, romance

[   ]My partner does not plan romantic dates, initiate sex, cuddle, act sensual

[   ]My partner shuts me out sexually or I shut my partner out sexually but there are reasons we have each lost interest, we keep each other at a distance usually

[   ]I feel depressed, am not interested in sex, don't want to be bothered

[   ]We can't "talk" and aren't very close so why have sex, it would only be forced

[   ]I feel guilty and obligated to have sex more than I want to and "it's never enough" anyway, and then I'm told I'm not "into it enough"...I can't win

[   ]My partner does not try to improve as a sexual lover: kiss romantically, caress, act sensual, is not nurturing, is usually critical of me, stays angry and demanding

[   ]Romance is just a fantasy, we just don't have time or money

[   ]My partner isn't much fun because he or she is: too serious, can't let go and relax, problems with addictions, has to stay compulsively busy/moving, is too anxious or worried, is often too angry to have fun, social issues, workaholic/ stays busy, too depressed, bickers too much, blames me and stays angry

[   ] I don't feel my partner wants a more intimate relationship with me

[   ] We have sex but we aren't "lovers" and we have settled for a relationship without much sexuality, passion or flirting

[   ] We have very little affection, touching, kissing, cuddling, loving and we keep each other at "arm's length" with bickering and moodiness

Journal about our ROMANCE AND SEXUALITY ISSUES

Name_____ Date_____

RE-BUILD EMOTIONAL TRUST
Getting and Receiving Feedback

WHY CAN'T WE OPEN UP TO EACH OTHER
- What do we each avoid talking about?
- Why can't we each "feel heard" at a deeper level?
- What needs to change for us to begin to talk more openly?

DATE/TIME WE TALKED_____

WHO INITIATED THIS TALK?_____

SOMETHING THAT KEEPS US "ON THE SURFACE"
- Take a risk! Bring up something you tend to ignore.
- Is one of us too moody? Is it a burden on our relationship?
- What "pushes each of us away"? Describe it, be specific.

DATE/TIME WE TALKED_____

WHO INITIATED THIS TALK?_____

NOURISH OUR RELATIONSHIP AS "LOVERS"
- What do we like to do as a couple for dates, romance?
- How would we act, feel if we went out "as lovers"?
- How could we both "get out of the box"? Have adventure?

DATE/TIME WE TALKED_____

WHO INITIATED THIS TALK?_____

Some tips to get deeper: Try to tolerate some discomfort and allow each other to open up about feelings you usually avoid. If you feel too defensive to be able to talk, then a couples session is the best option. If you stay agreeable and superficial, nit pick, or change the subject you aren't going to be able to make real changes in your relationship! Take a risk! Speak up and make a difference.

Name_____ Date_____

TO FEEL LIKE "LOVERS" YOU HAVE TO ACT LIKE IT!

Dating like "lovers" again
Learning to make simple, everyday things more fun
Learn how to make "EVERYDAY DATES FUN": just simple things

[ ]take a bath together and **soap each other**, not as foreplay, just to touch and play

[ ]cook a meal **together**; work in the kitchen; be playful and make it romantic!

[ ]watch a show together but **make it "special"**, cuddle, with wine and cheese

[ ]take a **"lover's walk"** around your neighborhood, feel like lovers not roommates

[ ]go **shopping together as "lovers"**, holding hands, being close, flirting together

[ ]walk on the beach, have a glass of wine, **watch the sunset**, talk romantic

[ ]take an **afternoon nap** together as "lovers", lying close and spoon

[ ]**kiss and hold** each other (even get "hot" but don't have sex! for now, anyway)

[ ]go for a drive but don't plan your destination, **have lunch somewhere new**

[ ]go **to a bookstore** and have coffee, read something you like to each other

[ ]visit **a pet store just for laughs** or take your pets to the park

[ ]sit out in the yard and **really "talk" about deep subjects** and carry the conversation

[ ]**get Chinese and sit on the floor** and eat, then lie there and cuddle

[ ]tell your partner **10 things you truly appreciate** about him/her;

[ ]**exercise together:** jog, walk, go to the gym, swim and be aware of each other's bodies

[ ]write a letter to your partner about **the relationship you envision** for both of you

[ ]ask your partner **to tell you 3 dates** he/she would love to go on; plan one together

[ ]go shopping and **point out gifts you would love** to each other (don't buy yet)

[ ]have an afternoon where you are **your partner's "slave"** and pamper him/her

[ ]give your partner a **deep massage for 15-20 minutes** and let him/her fall asleep

[ ]visit the nearby **art museum together** and "show it" to your partner

[ ]listen to **jazz, blues, or favorite music on a Sunday afternoon** but really be romantic while you do it, hold hands, cuddle, kiss

*Now talk together and plan a date. Try different things and "get out of the box" of routine. Don't find excuses not to date, find reasons to bring back the spark!

Name_____ Date_____

Have a "date" to feel close- to show affection- to be "lovers"

Each partner can take a turn initiating and planning a fun date. Bring some flirty, sexy, energy that makes it more than just "getting out together". Act like "lovers" not friends!!! Notice how lovers act and how they are very attentive to each other.

GETTING and GIVING FEEDBACK

- What was particularly difficult or uncomfortable for you? It **won't be "natural"** or you would already be doing it! How did you get past your resistance or procrastination? Look inside at why you have been stuck?

- How often do you and your partner **"date" each other** and really put effort into being "in your own world together", just the two of you?

- Is your date sensual and **do you flirt?** Do you show affection with touching? (Do you feel like "lovers" together?

- Do you try to **create the energy of passion** in the way you relate? Do you want to get this spark back into your relationship? Do you feel it's missing?

- What are you willing to do to **rekindle this spark?** Talk this over with your partner this week and write about it below. What are you willing to "give" to make your relationship better instead of staying stuck in anger?

- If nothing changes, **what is likely to happen in your relationship?** Are you expecting your partner to make all the changes? Are you willing to accept your 50% of the responsibility for why it has become a problem and...
  THEN DO SOMETHING TO MAKE SOME REAL CHANGES?

If your relationship is not as satisfying as you want it to be and not as sensual or romantic, what are 3 things you could do to improve this? Ask your partner!

1._____

_____

2._____

_____

3._____

_____

Name_____ Date_____

GROWING OUR RELATIONSHIP TOGETHER

PROGRAMMING
stuck in unhealthy
patterns

HEART-CENTERED LOVE

REPROGRAMMING
a higher level of
love

Communication and Feeling "Heard"

Week 6	Reprogramming Tools Exercises, Homework and Tools
Communication and Feeling "Heard"	• Showing some empathy, reflecting, supporting • Rate your partner, listening, "hearing" • Patterns that "end the communication" • Do you deny, avoid, pretend, or shut down? • Communication that builds Emotional Trust • Growing into more Emotional Maturity

COMMUNICATION & "FEELING HEARD"

Communication that is open and nourishing builds emotional trust, which improves the quality of relationships. When emotional trust is high partners feel they are **getting their needs met**. They feel close, warm, and loving. Today we have the tools to actually learn how to **raise the level of emotional trust** in our relationship.

When couples have low levels of emotional trust, **communication ends** because a partner controls it in some way. Attacking, venting, blaming, building a case, being right, getting violent, raging, threats, lectures, being a bully are **some active ways** to end the communication. Passive ways to end the communication are just as deadly. Some **passive ways** to end the communication are leaving, withdrawing and giving in, staying closed, making your partner "pull teeth", being a victim, "poor me", being too compliant (empty promises), and others. These patterns keep both partners from feeling emotionally nourished and close. The relationship stays on the surface. Sex and romance **lacks the depth of a mature relationship**. When partners can't communicate with depth, when communication ends because of unhealthy patterns, partners **don't "feel heard"**.

In many families we **didn't learn how to communicate** with empathy and support, to be open, to be nourishing to a partner. We may need to practice communicating in new ways. Unless communication has depth and both partners feel nourished and supported, the relationship will not become as close as we want it to. **Sex and romance are fragile**, delicate aspects of love and they flourish when partners have open hearts toward each other and their emotional trust is high. When a partner doesn't "feel heard", emotional trust isn't high, needs aren't being met, and **a "wall" will grow**. Sex and romance won't feel satisfying, it will start to feel forced, pressured, and controlled. Both partners need **to become a team** to grow out of this.

Healthy, **mature relationships are reciprocal**. Both partners try to nourish each other emotionally and put forth some effort in making changes. Immature relationships are based on the wounded child's emotional demands to make the relationship a one-way kind of nourishing, like childhood. The wounded child in a man may feel entitled to act out abuse, to stay adolescent and demanding sexually, may sabotage dating and nourishing his woman. His child wants her to be "his mother" so he won't want to flirt and be mature in how he nourishes her. A woman's wounded child will resist dating a man as a mature partner, being playful and healthy with him, making love to him, making him feel special and desired. She will want to lecture, criticize or see him in a negative way or sabotage in other ways. Non reciprocal relationships feel stuck and distant. The heart feels restless!

DIRECTIONS: One of us is the "talker" and opens up and talks about something for 5 minutes while the "listener" tries to show empathy, offer support, reflect back what's being said. Then we switch roles. The "listener" is supposed to practice really "hearing" the talker, not being defensive, changing the focus back to his/her feelings, or ending the communication by being mad. The "listener" may have to practice a few times to be a more nourishing partner.

1,2,3... "FEELING HEARD" EXERCISE
Improving our communication

1... REFLECT back what is being said

"What it sounds like you're really saying is (repeat points)..."

"It sounds like your point of view is (give a general summary)..."

"Could you talk about this some more, give me some details..."

"Could you give me some specific examples of how you feel..."

2... Show EMPATHY to your partner

"I can hear you and see what your feelings about this issue are..."

" Let me show you I understand it from your point of view ..."

"If I was in your shoes, I might feel similar to how you feel..."

"Looking at the big picture, considering what was going on..."

3... Offer SUPPORT to your partner

"What could I do now that would make a difference...?"

"What do you need from me in order for us to feel closer...?"

"Tell me some reasonable support that I could offer you..."

"I care how you feel and want you to feel I am a team..."

Do I "feel heard" and does my partner show caring and empathy for my feelings?

PRACTICING FOR 10 MINUTES

Practice the "FEELING HEARD" EXERCISE for 5 minutes each (use a timer) and reflect back what your partner says, show some *genuine empathy* for your partner's point of view, and offer some *reasonable support* in the way the exercise shows. Really "talk" and open up to each other instead of staying stuck "blaming" and "talking at" each other.

Key : GETTING & GIVING FEEDBACK WITH MY PARTNER

♥ Did I **reflect back** and really show you I heard your feelings and point of view (even if I don't agree)? Did you **feel heard** by me?

♥ Did I show some **empathy** for how you feel, for why you feel that way?

♥ Did I offer some **emotional support** even if I disagree?

GIVING FEEDBACK TO MY PARTNER

GETTING FEEDBACK TO MY PARTNER

Name_____ Date_____

Becoming a more
Emotionally Nourishing Partner!

We just can't "talk" anymore!"
We stay on the surface!

Use a timer and take turns. Just take 5 minutes each to learn new ways to show interest in your partner, even if you don't agree with his/her views.

It's just 10 minutes...

1. Learn to listen to each other for 5 minutes.

☐ "How do you feel about this? I want to know **how you feel**."

☐ "**Why do you feel** this way? What **causes you to feel** this way?"

☐ "What would you like for me **to do differently**? What could you do?"

☐ Use **Communication patterns** that show your partner you care and "hear" even if you don't agree. You will learn these in couples therapy.
Reflecting back, Showing Empathy, Offering Support

2. Ask for some feedback. Don't be defensive.

☐ "Did I **hear your feelings** and show you I understand your point of view?"

☐ "Did I Show you I was interested in your feelings."

☐ "Do you feel supported, nourished, or "heard" even if we disagree ?"

☐ "What could I do to make you feel more supported emotionally?"

3. Rate your partner's effort. Practice together!

Oops! 1   2   3   4   5   6   7   8   9   10 Great job!

Name_____ Date_____

Communication Patterns
that keep us Stuck

[ ]**"Being right"** staying rigid vs. compromise, being inflexible, too controlling, being an authority, quoting sources, being superior, lecturing

[ ]**"Building a Case"** making your partner wrong, being closed, not being open to your partner's feelings, exaggerating, staying angry

[ ]**"Being Adversarial"** not trying to be "on the same team", me not us, being controlling/demanding not inviting, working "against not with"

[ ]**"Power-Struggles"** trying to win is controlling, both of you can win, frequent bickering, hostility over small things not dealt with in mature ways, not trying to resolve concerns, passive-aggressive resistance to being a team

[ ]**"Excuses"** why it won't /can't work, why you won't try, finding reasons to stay stuck, instead of working at "making it happen" intimacy

[ ]**"Using Anger for Control"** staying too angry to listen, to try, to work at it, being innocent, feeling entitled to act out, to control with anger, being a bully, leaving the room, punishing, threatening to end the relationship

[ ]**"Blaming"** blaming your partner, not taking your part of the issue, staying "innocent", being unaware of your 50% of the issues, not owning your personal responsibility for why things feel tense, distant

[ ]**"Changing the focus"** avoiding the real issue, nitpicking with details, using the past to change the focus, counterattacks, getting off track, picking petty fights

[ ]**"My way is the only way"** not being open to partner's opinions, feelings, needs and suggestions, holding a rigid position, instead of being a team, not making compromises, negotiating, stuck in "all or none" thinking

[ ]**"If you loved me"** not saying what you want and making it a request, using guilt and pressure to get what you want, manipulation, pressure with your requests

[ ]**"You owe me"** being a martyr, "look at all I do for you", you should take care of my needs because you owe me for what I give to you/do for you, this is often a problem with sexual demands instead of sexual intimacy

[ ]**"Having the relationship in your head"** instead of saying what you feel, want, need directly you expect your partner to give it to you on your terms, reacting without open communication, analyzing instead of being open

[ ]**"My partner controls me"** it is a pattern you also have that works with your controlling partner, you are both locked in some angry feelings that keep getting acted out by staying stuck, being controlled is a pattern from childhood, you have chosen a controlling partner to act it out with

These patterns "end" the communication and it can't get deeper and help us resolve our issues.

WE DON'T GET ANYWHERE WHEN WE TALK!
Patterns to grow out of! These common patterns keep our communication from having depth and connection!

AVOIDING
Staying busy, being distracted, and filling up time is a way to avoid connection and intimacy. It's all about control and being detached emotionally. This keeps your partner at arm's length and your communication superficial. Higher love isn't about avoidance.

SHUTTING DOWN
If you shut down and eat, do drugs, drink too much, work or stay busy compulsively your whole life will feel like you are "missing something". Shutting down is a way of life to avoid buried feelings. No one can get close to you if you are very shut down and emotionally detached.

IMMATURE PATTERNS
Healthy, mature adult love is not about emotionally being needy, empty, desperate, clinging, caretaking, pleasing or a victim. These are patterns learned from your childhood. Any 14 year old kid can be needy and moody. Mature love is more nourishing than "acting out" these patterns.

IDEALIZING
Do you put your partner "on a pedestal", idealize your partner, make your partner feel "too wonderful, perfect, beautiful"? Does your partner tell you this is sort of sickening sometimes or feels too smothering? You are approaching your partner from your wounded child and it isn't attractive.

DENIAL
Do you deny problems ("Get over it! It was just a mood"), minimize the issues ("It was just one DUI and I don't have a drinking problem!"), or try to "normalize" things that are really important ("Lots of couples stop having sex, that's just how marriage is")? This keeps your life and love stuck!

BEING "ON"
Are you "on", "up", "fine" all the time? This is about control, being closed, and staying guarded emotionally. You only allow people to get close to the part of you that is excessively "in control". Often it takes addictions and compulsive issues to maintain this unhealthy façade. It's not open to love.

BUILDING EMOTIONAL TRUST
Isn't love worth it?
You base your whole life on it!

MOVE OUT OF BLAMING
TAKE MY 50% OF THE
RESPONSIBILITY

*Discuss a problem and take YOUR 50% of the emotional responsibility for this problem...THIS IS EMOTIONAL MATURITY

- **Show some empathy**
  "It must make you feel..."
- **Stop being adversarial**
  "How could we be a team?"
- **Be supportive to each other**
  "Did I also hear your feelings?"
- **Not ME,ME,ME-be reciprocal**
  "What are your needs too?"
- **Ask your partner for feedback**
  "What could I do different?"

Use your "ADULT" to set healthy, more mature BOUNDARIES and to invite and ask for REASONABLE EMOTIONAL NEEDS ...
EMOTIONAL TRUST IS VITAL TO LOVE...

STEP 1. Journal a relationship problem that left you both angry, distant, **BLAMING** each other, feeling far apart.

STEP 2. What is **MY OWN 50%** of this problem? What do you think you could you have done differently? This is maturity!

STEP 3. Shift into your adult to ask for **REASONABLE NEEDS**, set some healthy, mature **BOUNDARIES**, and communicate in your highest-functioning, mature **ADULT VOICE**

SHIFT into your ADULT (a tool) in order to get out
of the angry, blaming, wounded child and SHIFT INTO
MORE HEALTHY, MATURE COMMUNICATION

*Use journaling tools to begin to be more aware of how you are treating your partner, pushing your partner away, or staying stuck being distant.

- **Am I pushing my partner away?**
  Ask! Get some feedback. Open up communication.
- **How is my energy on our dates?**
  Am I inviting? Warm? Mature? Fun to be with?
- **How am I nourishing "us"?**
  How do I nourish my partner? Ask for feedback!
- **How open am I emotionally?**
  Am I closed? Defensive? Controlling? Too many excuses? Do I react righteous and "innocent"?
- **What kind of partner am I?**
  Ask my partner. Get feedback. Talk about it openly.

EVIDENCE SHOWS
Couples who put the effort into writing and journaling make more changes than those who just talk about changes!
or make **TEMPORARY, SUPERFICIAL CHANGES.**

JOURNAL about our communication and emotional trust...including my own 50% of the responsibility for staying emotionally distant, stuck or superficial. What's keeping me from making healthy changes? **What do I want and need from my partner in order to feel closer and be more reciprocal? What does my partner need from me?**

Name _____   Date_____

GROWING INTO EMOTIONAL MATURITY

We **didn't grow up with role models** for healthy, vibrant emotional closeness so in many cases we simply lack these skills. All **we feel are the symptoms** of our relationship when it's non-reciprocal, distant, or unnourishing. These symptoms often fit into the profiles of the **roommates or the bickering-adversarial couples**. These aren't the causes, just the symptoms. Trying to fix the symptoms takes a long time and usually isn't as effective as working on growing into more mature, healthy patterns together. Many couples get married young and aren't skilled in the patterns a higher level of love is built upon. You can grow into being **a more emotionally mature partner!**

[   ] **I try to open up the communication** and when it ends I hang in there. I give feedback to my partner and ask for feedback to make real changes. I want the depth of real communication. I am growing out of triggered reactions, blaming, and unhealthy patterns.

[   ] **I am taking some (my 50%) of the responsibility** for making changes. Taking responsibility isn't just verbal, it is making changes to show my partner I want a healthier level of love.

[   ] **I am growing to be a more mature, reciprocal partner.** I plan dates, am open to new, more mature, intimate dates. I am not in a rut. I take the initiative and want to be a lover to my partner. I expect mature nourishment on our dates.

[   ] **I do not perpetuate my wounded child's patterns** of keeping my partner at a distance. (men) I do not use my partner as a "mother" to the child in me. (women) I do not push my man away and turn him into a parent, not a partner.

[   ] **My lifestyle is healthy enough** and I am not stuck in using my relationship as a crutch, a hide-out, as the only thing in my life. This is too dependent and unhealthy. I am taking steps to build a healthier lifestyle. I try new things!

[   ] **My triggered reactions, negative moods, aren't a burden.** I manage my moods and make a real effort to bring some fun, warmth, nourishment to my partner when we spend quality time together.

Put a √ on the boxes my partner wants me to work on.
Name_____ Date_____

GROWING OUR RELATIONSHIP TOGETHER

PROGRAMMING
stuck in unhealthy patterns

HEART-CENTERED LOVE

REPROGRAMMING
a higher level of love

Core wounds are our "Baggage"

Week 7	Reprogramming Tools Exercises, Homework and Tools
Core Wounds are our "Baggage"	• Core Wounds are our "Baggage"! • What are our Core Wounds? • How do core wounds interfere with love? • Our Weakest Link is our "baggage"

CORE WOUNDS KEEP US STUCK

Core wounds are common, everyone has a few. They make us all unique and build character. They also persist into adult life and keep recycling in spite of the fact that you've grown up and forgotten about their causes. Unfortunately they're the **least healthy part of us** and are filled with old anger, pain, sadness, and emotions we couldn't deal with as a child. By the time we're adults **we aren't in touch with these old wounds**, and only become aware of them when **we get moody and triggered**. Some people get triggered and **overreact** with too much anger. Others have **triggered moods** like feelings of intense loneliness, or pockets of depression that really aren't even caused by your adult life today. Still other people have reactions filled with anxiety or insecurity that reflects old feelings from childhood more than who you are now. Keeping core wounds buried is a **childhood strategy for coping** with feelings because young children don't know how to deal with them. As adults burying and stuffing our feelings isn't a healthy strategy because it really doesn't get rid of them. Buried feelings keep us too detached, too compulsive (being busy all the time is a defense), or addictive. They can even make us sick with too much stress. They cause us to have moods, triggered reactions, and projections that interfere with love. We can use tools to **identify and release the buried feelings** stored in core wounds.

Triggered core wounds usually cause **communication to stay stuck.** A partner who reacts with too much **anger over small slights** is triggered. A partner who can't communicate and is **unable to be open** is being triggered. A partner who has to **control, nitpick, and is critical** is triggered. A **passive, compliant partner** is triggered. A partner who gets triggered as **a victim or a martyr** probably has a core wound to deal with. As you look over some of these common examples of core wounds it's easy to see how they interfere with communication.

Today we have tools to grow out of core wounds and to **release the toxic buried feelings they store.** When we start to recognize our own 2-3 irrational, intense, triggered reactions or moods we can use the healthier part of our personality to deal with them. An easy way to conceptualize this is to think of core wounds, caused and buried during childhood, as those **triggers stored in the wounded child.** The healthier, more mature part of our personality is called the adult and we can use it to manage core wounds. We can actually **shift into our adult** and then support, guide, nurture the child. We can use the adult to voice the child's needs and feelings instead of allowing the child to vent, blame, attack, punish and act out, which ruins love. Using tools to shift brings more **emotional responsibility and maturity to love.** The **adult is a tool** to release buried feelings in core wounds.

Do CORE WOUNDS get triggered?

Some of my moods keep getting triggered and interfere with my relationship.

[ ] I tend to have low energy too often, I push myself or feel collapsed

[ ] I feel moody, lonely inside, or empty, can't "be alone and just feel ok"

[ ] I feel hurt too easily, feel rejected, am too sensitive, get defensive

[ ] I feel compulsive, pressured, have to stay busy, running, doing

[ ] I can use sex as a "fix", I don't get close more mature, healthy ways

[ ] I use threats, have a short fuse, use anger for control, can be a bully

[ ] I can be self-centered, "it's all about me", even "talk at" not "with"

[ ] I can be demanding for attention, I can be needy with negative moods

[ ] I feel empty, flat, blah, numb, wound up or bored when I slow down

[ ] I am passive, dependent, "waiting", feel like life is "out there"

[ ] I feel unmotivated, don't have goals, can't self-start, I'm in a rut

[ ] I feel like I have to keep my guard up, can't get close to people

[ ] I tend to "buy" love, I get used, taken for granted, give too much

[ ] I do a million things but nobody "gets in", I am busy, in control

[ ] I get angry easy and vent sometimes, I overreact to small things

[ ] I feel overwhelmed by everyday things, daily life feels hard

[ ] I feel insecure, I keep my partner "on a leash", I expect check-ins

[ ] Life isn't fun, I live in a box, everything is routine, no real adventures

Name _____ Date_____

Some of the causes of Core Wounds

Most people have between 2-3 **CORE WOUNDS** that get triggered as a mood or emotional reaction. These are usually "out of context" in your life today, don't make sense within the adult life you have now. These are caused by experiences from your past that surface today, even though you have now forgotten what really caused them. Everyone has their own unique history and experiences that isn't identical to anyone else. Your specific core wound will be unique to you, to your background and history. However most people have experienced some **GENERAL** experiences that are similar, caused by these type of life-altering, damaging experiences.

CORE WOUND CAUSED BY ABANDONMENT, NEGLECT, or REJECTION ...
[   ] I was left alone for long periods of time, told to be good, play by myself
[   ] I had a parent abandon me emotionally, just disappear from our relationship abruptly
[   ] My parent was self-absorbed, even when we were together it was not nurturing to me
[   ] My parent acted too busy, too preoccupied or too stressed to relate with me much
[   ] My parent was emotionally shut down, distant, or even cold toward me, not warm
[   ] I rarely recall times when my parent looked to me with love and warmth for me
[   ] I didn't feel wanted, adored, special and my parent didn't make time for me, for us
[   ] My basic needs (food, shelter, stuff) were provided for but I felt alone, not connected
[   ] We didn't talk much, we didn't share, I never felt much interest or encouragement in me
[   ] My parent didn't feel "mothering" or "fathering" toward me, I was "just there"

CORE WOUND CAUSED BY BEING CRITICIZED, PRESSURED, or SMOTHERED...
[   ] I was special and knew Mom and Dad depended on me "to win", to make them winners
[   ] From and early age I was told how I would fulfill Mom's/Dad's dreams, goals
[   ] I was Mama's boy, even more special than Dad; I was Daddy's girl and Mom was jealous
[   ] I was Mom's best friend, we did a lot together; Dad and I did all "his things" as buds
[   ] My parent was critical, pressured me, pointed out my mistakes often, judged me
[   ] I rarely recall times when my parent told me all the wonderful things about me
[   ] I didn't feel special, talented in my own right, and wasn't nurtured to fulfill my potential
[   ] My basic needs (food, shelter, stuff) were provided for but I wasn't helped, given time
[   ] I never felt much interest or encouragement in my world, but there was always pressure
[   ] We didn't have long talks about what I like, was curious about, thought was important

SPECIFIC CORE WOUNDS CAUSED BY EARLY TRAUMA and NOT FEELING SAFE...
[   ] I was left alone for long periods of time, told to be good, play by myself
[   ] I had a parent abandon me emotionally, just disappear from my life abruptly
[   ] My parent was self-absorbed, didn't think about what was good for a kid's best interest
[   ] My parent acted too busy, too preoccupied or too stressed and had a lot of good excuses
[   ] My parent was cold toward me, abusive or too moody to feel safe with; I was scared
[   ] Our home life was unpredictable, calm one minute and explosive or full of drama suddenly
[   ] We had serious addictions, mental illness or emotional problems that kept us all on edge
[   ] My parent was too needy, controlling and made me take care of her/his adult problems
[   ] I wasn't protected from abuse, from being used, or from sexually inappropriate behavior
[   ] I got about as much care and attention as our dog; I felt I had to be strong and not need

Most people have between 2-3 CORE WOUNDS that get triggered as a mood or emotional reaction. These are usually "out of context" in your life today, don't make sense within the adult life you have now. These are caused by experiences from your past that surface today, even though you have now forgotten what really caused them. Everyone has their own unique history and experiences that isn't identical to anyone else. Your specific core wound will be unique to you, to your background and history. However most people have experienced some GENERAL experiences that are similar, caused by these type of life-altering, damaging experiences.

CORE WOUND CAUSED BY ABANDONMENT, NEGLECT, or REJECTION ...

Parents who were uninvolved with you, kept you at arm's length, weren't emotionally nurturing to you, didn't bond with you, were abusive, or weren't "there" for you in important ways will cause you to have a core wound inside that feels empty, lonely, rejected, depressed, even angry. Your particular symptoms depend on what you experienced. Generally latch key children, kids who are reinforced to be alone, children who were abused and not "parented" by self-absorbed parents learned not to expect much nurturing. They usually have compulsive and addictive issues as adults. These adults may stay detached from these wounded feelings by living on the surface, "in their head". Many people have unconscious programming to recreate this same distance, neglect, abuse and rejection and are attracted to partner's who treat them this way. Childhood programmed you with the patterns for this level of "love".

CORE WOUND CAUSED BY BEING CRITICIZED, PRESSURED, or SMOTHERED...

Parents who weren't emotionally nurturing to you, didn't support your talents, gifts, dreams, and didn't encourage you to explore your own strengths weren't "there" for you in important ways. Parents who were "smothering", lived through a child too much, or were too dependent on a child (used them for "friends", "therapists", built their life around a child) prevent their child from developing as healthy separate, whole people. They may later look for another controlling partner. Some parents have critical, rigid, or perfectionist issues that made a child feel "I can never do it right", "nothing I do gets recognized", "the things I'm good at aren't important". Being overly pressured, criticized causes a wound inside that feels insecure, empty, worthless, pressured or angry. Your particular symptoms depend on what you experienced. Being smothered or molded in rigid critical ways causes core wounds.

SPECIFIC CORE WOUNDS CAUSED BY EARLY TRAUMA and NOT FEELING SAFE...

Parents who didn't provide a safe relationship that you could lean on may not have made you feel you could go to them when "scary, bad things" were happening. Children who tolerate years of violence and rage, serious addictive acting out, chaos, constant drama, abuse, molestation, not having a stable home life, or other trauma learned not to reach out for protection, support, guidance, and safety. As adults these same patterns are still going on and the person tolerates many boundary violations, lack of mature behavior in a partner, and many of the same neglect, excuses, they originally experienced. Trauma is bad enough and leaves scars on a child but even more insidious is the child's view of the world where this awful thing is happening and everyone is too busy, too preoccupied, too self-centered, and just "not there" to deal with it alongside their child. Adults have core wounds from this.

A Few Examples of CORE WOUNDS

Core wounds don't go away, they persist and keep on recycling in our adult personality even if they seem irrational to us now. We have grown out of the causes of them but the old buried feelings are festering and need to be released. Core wounds are those "triggered moods" that seem like they've always been there. They were caused by problems in your childhood or you inherited them from your parent's personalities. Here are some examples of some people who have identified some core wounds. See if you can relate to these examples. Abuse, neglect, and not being nurtured causes addictive or compulsive issues and people tend to be shut down, to "live in their head". You'll notice these same symptoms again and again because they're common. They keep you from being a healthy, nourishing partner in higher level love.

"neglected" child

I am used to being ignored at a deep level. I ignore my needs and feelings and others ignore them too. I stay on the surface, feel something is missing, feel empty inside when I slow down. I'm strong and "fine"!

SYMPTOMS
- I feel empty, wound up when I slow down instead of relaxed, calm, full, at peace
- I feel needy for someone to be with, I don't like to be alone, I have to stay busy
- I stay disconnected, I numb myself, tend to medicate myself so I don't slow down
- I stay "fine, up" but am irritable, have an angry edge or feel tired, bored
- I live "in my head" and no one gets close, nothing "gets in"
- Mom was too stressed so I tried to stay out of the way and not be a burden
- Dad was drinking a lot and into his own moods; he didn't seem to like kids

a successful business owner

"controlling" child

I was deprived as a child and my feelings surface as impulses, cravings, and I feel I have to do something, give myself something, I am impulsive, controlling and demanding. Food is all I have! I am so "in my head" and "in control" I can't get nourished in other ways.

SYMPTOMS
- I want it right now, I don't want to wait! I feel impulsive, anzty, I need something
- I stuff my feelings, have cravings
- I live in my head, I pressure myself
- I feel empty, bored, when I slow down, but I avoid it usually
- when I feel needy I may use some substances to comfort, soothe my feelings
- I feel ok when I stay busy, doing, disconnected from these feelings
- I get filled up from caretaking others, doing fillers, I am often over-extended
- I may feel depressed, tired, or empty and then become angry, irritable, or pick a fight with a family member
- I stay in control and get up and do it again
- I'm a bit of Superwoman, a perfectionist

a busy Mom who over-extends

"all about me" child

I wasn't close to Mom and wasn't the center of her attention, of her love. I want to be listened to, have my partner be my audience. I tell stories. I brag, and talk "all about me".

SYMPTOMS

- I didn't get enough attention as a child, I feel hungry inside, needy for strokes
- I have trouble feeling OK, relaxed, just being at ease, feel wound up inside
- I stay busy, feel stressed, am disconnected, in my head, am a workaholic
- I'm a bit demanding for the focus to be "all about me", my dreams, accomplishments
- I numb myself, zone out with TV, computer
- I'm irritable underneath but blame my moods on wife, kids most of the time
- My father was moody, angry, scared me
- I need an audience, make my friends, my wife listen, nurture me, give me strokes

a professional man

"good and busy" child

My parents liked me to be good, not need anything, not be a bother, and I feel a lot of inner pressure to stay busy. I am compulsive to keep doing things. I can be too serious. I have "lists" in my head, I'm rigid, shut down.

SYMPTOMS

- I don't slow down, I stay productive, I am in control and I do it all
- When I feel needy I don't get in touch with it, stay very busy, have a "to do" list
- I feel pressure to be compulsive, do more, be perfect, to be the "best"
- I rarely have fun, I am too serious, like a "little adult"
- I have a "wall" and live in my head, no one gets in
- I'm moody if I slow down, I feel empty so I don't, I stay "on, up, fine"
- I only connect by having someone need me, lean on me and I get used, feel bitter

an executive woman

"rebellious" child

I didn't learn to lean on, trust, feel safe with authorities (parents) as a child. I have an angry edge. I can be a bully. People "walk on eggshells" around me. I'm aggressive, sarcastic, put people down. I'm negative.

SYMPTOMS

- I have a chip on my shoulder, I'm mad at authority
- I am wound up, disconnected, moody and irritable
- I ignore my feelings, feel bored, flat, empty but use substances or women
- I "act out", can "look for a fight", can be self destructive or vindictive
- I never learned to lean, trust, feel safe, don't give up control to anyone
- No one has ever been there for me, no one "gets in" much, and I tell people that
- My partner "walks on eggshells"

a self-employed business owner

"seductive" child

I don't get filled up and use my charm to stay in control, get a "fix" of attention, comfort. When I'm not needy I am not close to people at a deep level. People don't "get in" very much except when I need attention.

SYMPTOMS

- When I feel bored , I can become impulsive, needy and want sex, to flirt, to chat seductively but don't have love in my life
- I stay busy, disconnected, don't know what I really need, I can use sex compulsively
- I feel lonely inside and sexualize it when I need some attention, but then feel used
- I distract myself, avoid core feelings, am needy with a "fix", don't feel nourished
- I don't get close in real ways with people, don't have much connection, I stay distant
- I stay on the surface, am fun, on, strong, in control, charming and seem ok

a professional woman

"loner" child

I learned how to stay in control and be alone, I need and want to be taken care of like "an adolescent" by my partner not a healthy adult. I make my partner a "parent" more than an equal partner.

SYMPTOMS

- I like to zone out, stay disconnected and don't feel much, just flat line usually
- I seem to crave my addiction and can't get sober; I have trouble sleeping
- I have a few beers every day to get by
- I don't let people in, close, keep them at arm's length, they know the strong me
- I often feel lonely, but am so used to it, I just distract myself, I stay busy all the time
- I'm angry, irritable, have angry or depressed moods, or stay compulsive
- I am isolated and only let in "safe" people I can control, my world is a small box
- My wife nags a lot and has gained weight so I'm not attracted to her any more
- Porn is more fun and no one talks back

a manager

"angry, venting" child

I am out of touch with myself, act out my needs by being angry. I don't get attention until I'm angry, not in healthy ways. I blow when it builds up. I feel empty when I slow down so I don't. I act nice on the surface but with an edge. I don't get close in nourishing ways.

SYMPTOMS

- I feel edgy more than most other emotions, moods but I act nice on the surface
- if I feel needy I don't know it, I feel irritable and edgy (not needy)
- I stay busy, disconnected, "up" and in control, don't know I need anything
- People close to me "walk on eggshells", they feel my angry edge
- I build a case and want my own way right now, I feel entitled
- I feel flat, empty, tired, or drained when I'm not getting attention for my moods
- I stay on the surface, am in control, I am demanding emotionally

a teacher

"scared, anxious child"

I am scared a lot of the time but I try to hide it so no one can tell. My Dad beat me a lot and beat Mom. I was criticized and pressured to do my best but mostly told how I could have done better. I get angry when I'm depressed.

SYMPTOMS
- I feel edgy more than most other emotions, moods but I act nice on the surface
- I stay busy, disconnected, "up" and in control, don't know I need anything
- People close to me "walk on eggshells", they feel my angry edge but underneath I am trying to be perfect all the time
- I feel flat, empty, tired, or drained when I'm not getting attention for my moods
- I stay on the surface, am in control, I am demanding emotionally
- My wife knows I'm too sensitive so she stays clear of me usually

a college professor

"insecure, not good enough" child

I feel "not good enough" most of the time but I try to hide it so no one can tell. I feel insecure when I am close to someone, and need a lot of reassurance or I choose a partner I feel won't leave me. I compare myself with others mentally and feel "less than."

SYMPTOMS
- I feel insecure and anxious to please but it's too much, I'm 'too nice' sometimes
- I stay busy, disconnected, "up" and in control, don't need anything
- People say I apologize a little too much
- My girlfriend has to reassure me she won't find someone better
- I stay on the surface, am in control, I am demanding emotionally for reassurance
- I feel anxious if someone gets mad and then I try too hard to please and to fix it
- I hate being "weak" like this and beat myself up about being so needy
- The only time I feel ok is when I have had a few drinks so I can relax and not sweat it

car salesman

"traumatic, secrets child"

I have dreams, memories or have blanked out years. I know things weren't right. I'm not sure. But I have a lot of symptoms that get in the way of my adult life. I never could lean on my parents about much.

SYMPTOMS
- I stay busy, disconnected, "up" and in control, don't know I need anything
- I am trying to be perfect, to get more done, to do it better all the time
- I feel flat, empty, tired, or drained when I'm not on the surface, in control
- I'm sensitive and creative but it leaves me "running on empty" and unnourished
- I have migraines, anxiety, and get depressed for no reason
- I am very wound up and uptight inside and my husband says it keeps me from being "in the mood"
- I feel my husband is too needy and it's a turn off; he has rages occasionally

artist-gallery owner

Identifying your own CORE WOUNDS

Your own unique experiences shape what feelings and moods you have inside that get triggered in your adult life today. Using these fairly general examples from other people you can see how common these wounds are. Most everyone has 2 or 3 wounds. As you explore your CORE WOUNDS and get a handle on why/how you sometimes react in ways that cause problems you'll notice these reactions aren't from your highest-functioning self! In many cases they **feel irrational** because they don't reflect the growth you have in the highest-functioning part of your personality. As you identify your emotional "baggage" you'll be able to use tools to help heal it. You can give yourself some healthier options besides acting it out in your adult relationship! Using tools for core wounds helps you heal them, release toxic feelings, and stop being a burden on love!

DIRECTIONS: Work with a therapist or use self-reflection to become aware of triggered moods and intense reactions that interfere with your relationship and your well being. They are often intense, overreactions and they are persistent, they recycle and repeat. We all have a few! They cause negative moods and intense triggered reactions.

My Triggers, Moods & Core Wounds	Describe my "baggage" & Wounded Moods	What in my past caused these Buried Feelings
neglected child "in my own world"		
controlling child can't lean, trust		
it's "all about me", needy for attention		

good and busy pressured child		
rebellious, bully, chip-on-my-shoulder		
feels used, needy seductive child		
bored, wound-up, numb, loner child		
angry-venting demanding child		

scared-anxious lonely child		
insecure, "not good enough" child		
traumatic, secret things in my past		
my own triggers and overreactions		
negative moods that keep recycling		

Name_____ Date_____

IS YOUR "WOUNDED CHILD" RUNNING YOUR LIFE?

MY "ADULT"
is the highest-functioning part of my personality

THE ADULT part of the personality is actually a tool used to **SHIFT** out of wounded feelings, moods, triggers, and negative reactions and beliefs your wounded child is programmed with. Which part of the personality do I want to run my life? The **ADULT** is a tool but it **has to be strengthened and reprogrammed in** order to use it effectively. Tools will help you shift to the highest-functioning part of yourself, to shift into your **ADULT** naturally!

MY "ADULT"
has an ADULT
VOICE to express
needs and feelings

What is a mood I feel fairly often? What is it about? What am I reacting to? How do I react when I feel this? What triggers it for me? How do I act it out usually? (ask your partner). The child is our raw reactions, impulses, our moods, buried feelings, triggers...and it's usually immature and self-absorbed.

a negative, anxious mood
acted out by: anxiety, being negative or stuck

an angry, "venting" mood
acted out by: picking a fight, staying blaming

a depressed mood
acted out by: being tired, "blah", edgy, wound up

a needy, lonely mood
acted out by: "waiting" or by being demanding

staying closed, compulsively busy
acted out by: being "on the surface", excuses

CORE WOUNDS are caused by BURIED FEELINGS-WOUNDED CHILD REACTIONS

I can't talk - I vent, nag, blame or complain

My anger gets triggered -it escalates fast

I stay on the surface, closed-I have a "wall"

I feel rejected-I get mad to get some attention

I don't feel wanted, cherished, or "good enough"

I feel needy-I may be clingy, beg, "buy", or obsess

I feel stuck-fear holds me back-I can't go forward

I get irritated-I am wound up tight-I have an edge

I am "waiting"- in fantasy- "the one" will save me

I'm passive-my partner has to push, prod, nag me

I need to rescue-to be in control-to be needed, a hero

I get used-I am seductive-men only want sex

Tools can be used to shift out of these core wounds!

Core wounds are old, immature beliefs and attitudes you formed as a child. They store buried feelings from past like anger, anxiety, pain, old loneliness. They are even pockets of fear, insecurity, negative thinking. They can cause you to need to stay in control excessively, to have irrational triggered emotional reactions, to hold limiting beliefs about yourself, people, love or life. Core wounds are your emotional "baggage"! They can hold you back.

Are we Attached at our Weakest Link?

Are we "AT RISK" for infidelity, divorce, or feeling stuck and distant?

My issues	Partner's issues	Are we connected with our emotional "baggage"? Do Core Wounds cause problems for us?
		I feel "used", taken for granted, taken advantage of by my partner. I give too much and resent it. I don't feel appreciated. It drains me.
		Sex can feel like a pressure sometimes and then my partner wants it again right away. This is a turn off. I don't feel very attracted now.
		We don't have enough fun, romance, playfulness and don't "date" each other, flirt! Sex is a little boring. We go out just to do something.
		I feel controlled by my partner, like I can't be free, and I feel like I'm "on a leash". I have to check in, call, text many times a day.
		Some serious painful things happened in my past. I have secrets that interfere with my relationship. I keep them under wraps, guarded.
		I have anger issues, road rage, a temper, may have some buried anger and have to really try to keep it under control. I get depressed from it.
		I take care of my partner who doesn't have a good job(or a car, saved money, doesn't plan for things). I feel needed. I'm a "rescuer."
		Since starting our relationship I rarely spend time with my friends, my partner demands almost all my time. I guess this is love?
		My whole life is centered around my relationship. I don't have much of a personal life of my own. I do everything with/for my partner.
		My partner controls me by pouting, acting sullen or getting mad, can be a bully. I give in and try to "fix it". I have sex, do what's expected.
		I stay busy or I'm compulsive about activities: computer, exercise, porn, food, TV, gambling, shopping... I am busy or distracted.
		I am busy, rarely slow down, then get up and do it all again. I run "on empty" most of the time. I feel stressed, wound up inside, or I crash.
		I don't have any real dreams of my own or personal goals I'm jazzed about working toward. My partner demands too much of my time.
		I feel moody, down, tired, sort of empty when I'm alone, by myself so I call someone, get busy, fill the time. I only feel ok when I'm busy.
		I express my needs with anger, have an "edge", can be bossy and feel I am entitled to get what I want. I'm opinionated, strong-willed.

		I like to be right, can feel righteous, can be a bit of a know-it-all, but I have my facts in order. I lecture, ramble, "talk at" my partner.
		I have given up important parts of my personality, and my life, in order to be in this relationship. I wish I had more in my life than I do.
		I've shut down sexually, ignore/avoid sex, use excuses and want a "roommates" relationship, don't desire sex. My partner complains.
		We have the "perfect marriage" on the surface, we each pretend it's ok, we deny, ignore many issues. We live on the surface, aren't open.
		My partner uses anger to intimidate me, is angry a lot and takes it out on me, "acts it out" in our relationship. There's always something!
		My partner doesn't put effort into being a healthy, sexual partner by creating desire, romance, fun, and attraction. It's just an expectation.
		My partner isn't any fun, doesn't flirt, play, act very alive and we're usually bored, tired, distant together. We don't have any romance.
		My partner uses problems with the kids to avoid a real adult romantic relationship. It's all we ever talk about! My partner's life is errands!
		I secretly think about having an affair because I feel I can't ever get my needs met with this partner. I don't talk about it. I won't leave.
		If I was financially independent or wouldn't lose too much financially, I'd probably leave this relationship. I feel trapped in some ways.
		We aren't close. My partner needs me, I need my partner. It would be too hard to start all over. I've never tried to make it better.
		We bicker, say rude things, put each other down, or lecture at each other. One of us is angry a lot. This is our main way to connect.
		I can never do enough, be good enough to please my partner. I try hard to please. There's always something wrong with me.
		I am too nice, try to please, tend to say "yes" and give a lot to others, too much sometimes. There's not much left over for a relationship.
		I need my partner but don't feel close and we have a silent "wall" between us, stay superficial, busy. My partner feels boring to me.
		Our relationship centers on chores, responsibilities, kids. We've lost that real male-female connection. We aren't attracted to each other.
		I feel scattered, unfocused, stressed and have no time or energy for my dreams. I've put most of my goals on hold. I do for others, give too much, am always focused on "helping" not on my goals, dreams.
		My relationship is like a hide out for me, to isolate in, and in some ways it's a crutch emotionally. Well, no one's perfect! I need it!

		I can't talk to my partner because I get lectured, a guilt trip, put down, criticized, or controlled in some way. I shut up, give up.
		My partner doesn't know the real me, my feelings, my needs, who I am. I have to be "on", "up", "fine". I am strong, am in control.
		My partner is a bully, acts critical, controlling, overbearing. She/he feels entitled to do this, doesn't try to bring a good energy or attitude.
		I have a lot of excuses for why I feel stuck in my life. I do what I have to, then zone out (TV, computer), distract myself when I have time off.
		I keep my partner at arm's length and have one foot out the door. My partner is insecure, jealous. I sometimes threaten to leave, divorce.
		I was controlled too much as a child and now my partner controls me all over again. I'm mad inside! I'm too much a "good girl/nice guy".
		I'm not attracted to my partner because he/she feels boring, needy, too dependent on me. I've lost respect. My partner's too boring, dull.
		My partner is sick a lot. Always some ache or pain, even the "real ones" are used to get attention, to stay in his/her shell, to avoid life.
		My partner doesn't dress up so we can go have fun, doesn't try to be attractive for me, won't take care of his/her body. I resent it.
		I am not very affectionate in mature ways, I'm not sexy, flirty with my partner. I stay aloof, distant, busy. I use work/the kids as an excuse.
		My partner acts "single" even though we're a couple. I feel like I have no say, no power, can't make decisions, am not treated equal.
		My partner doesn't cheat but is not available to spend any quality time with me. There's always something more important.
		I feel like a child with this partner, am not respected, feel talked down to, get bossed around. I have to take it but I simmer inside with anger.
		We fight, bicker, argue, and feel angry often. I can get really upset, yell, throw things, even get physical! I can't talk without getting mad!
		I have to give in to keep the peace and get along, just stuff it and wait until the next incident or blow up. It only gets worse if I speak up.
		I don't try to "talk" and solve fights any more, I ignore them, because it escalates very quick when we communicate. I don't feel "heard".
		I deny, minimize, rationalize it, pretend it's no big deal but our life is built around my addiction. My partner wishes I'd get some help.
		I feel uncomfortable being alone, want my partner to be together most of the time, and can be demanding. When I'm alone I feel "blah".
		When we're apart I usually call my partner many times a day just to "check in". I need to connect often. I get anxious if I can't connect.

Do Core Wounds keep our relationship stuck?

- Negative moods are a burden on our relationship and we are often dealing with "heavy moods", negativity, complaining

- We don't try new things, date, have enough fun, flirt, feel "light" and play together as a couple, don't have adventures

- We stay at a distance as "roommates" but feel unfulfilled, unsatisfied, lack passion, even feel resentful or bored

- We fight, argue, or bicker over everyday things too often and this keeps us on edge, at a distance, having power-struggles

- We struggle with addictions or compulsive issues and tolerate unhealthy dependency, denial, excuses, empty promises without real commitment to making changes

- We live crisis-to-crisis, it's always some drama we have to deal with, we don't feel calm, stable, relaxed as a family

- We stay "on the surface" usually and just connect when we are needy for attention, we aren't open at a deeper level

- We "go through the motions", feel that "something is missing" like we are stuck in a routine or a rut

Some Examples of Core Wounds

age 5- BAD-LOSER WOUND
- feel bad, wrong, stupid, lazy
- anxious, never feel safe, ok
- pressured to be perfect
- feel criticized a lot, on edge
- "not good enough"
- angry, guarded, defensive
- doesn't try new things
- feels insecure, empty
- always alone with a maid
- couldn't nap in kindergarten

age 7-LONER-LONELY WOUND
- doesn't "belong" anywhere
- shy, self-conscious, anxious
- uncomfortable with people
- doesn't feel accepted
- expects to be rejected
- angry, guarded, defensive
- tries too hard, gets drained
- overeats, gamer, movies
- isolates, "safe friends"
- has to drink to sleep, unwind

**the child
at my
CORE**

age 5- ROBOT-SERIOUS WOUND
- "to do" list, stays detached
- lives "in my head", not "here"
- wound up, uptight, anxious
- compulsively busy, stressed
- responsible, serious, rushed
- angry or depressed, a martyr
- codependent with others
- empty, needy, when alone
- can't relax or have fun
- isn't spontaneous or creative
- can't "play", let go, isn't free

A Professional Woman with Stress

This educated professional woman has been troubled by these 3 core wounds. They have held her back from being close to people. Because she felt so criticized inside, she hid it by taking care of others, by staying compulsively busy all the time. She couldn't relax and go to a movie. She wouldn't lean on anyone emotionally, or let others "get in" and she picked men who she could control, who leaned on her. She got "needy" in an unattractive, unbalanced way and only when she was in a seriously negative mood. This kept her from being nourished. She is tense most of the time and has high blood pressure from stress caused by feeling this way. People are turned off by intense neediness caused when someone isn't open, warm and half-full. She used tools to heal these immature wounds so she could be more open and less wound up in her life. These wounds limited her peace and joy. These wounds are not the highest-functioning part of her personality. It's such a shame to be limited by the wounds from our childhood. Using tools we can change these worn out defenses that hold us back! They also cause health issues when we stay so wound up or angry. She is so stressed she often feels sick or has unspecified aches and pains, is tired a lot.

age 5- "NEVER GOOD ENOUGH"
- I've always felt insecure
- I look for reassurance from my partner, I need too much
- I feel criticized , on edge
- I feel I'm "not good enough"
- I feel wrong, dumb, different
- I never feel I'm just ok
- I feel pressured to be better
- I'm guarded, defensive
- I don't try many things
- I feel empty when I slow down and get antsy inside
- I can't sleep, nightmares

age 13-MY ADDICT WOUND
- I use pot, drugs, get high often
- I'm wound up, uptight, anxious
- I stay compulsively busy, doing
- I'm angry inside, I'm moody
- I feel empty, needy, when I'm alone so I tune it all out
- I have fun, relax when I'm high
- I can't "play", let go unless I use something to unwind with
- I'm "on-up", have confidence when I get high, I fit in
- I feel numb, dead, flatline, bored unless I use

the child
at my
CORE

age9 – SOCIAL ANXIETY WOUND
- I'm self-conscious socially
- I watch myself, censor myself
- I feel judged, uncomfortable
- I have to try too hard
- I feel drained, want to hide
- I'm codependent with others
- I feel empty, needy, anxious and depressed when alone
- can't relax or have fun
- I'm not spontaneous or free
- I can't "play", let go, feel ok
- I'm careful, guarded, tense

A Man Who Can't Get Sober

This successful man has been troubled by these 3 core wounds and they have held him back from being close to people, from making friends, from feeling nourished in healthy ways. He feels so criticized inside because of his alcoholic, abusive mother, he hides it by being aloof, taking care of others, and being "on". He doesn't let anyone get too close or really "get in", wasn't close to anyone growing up and isn't used to closeness. He actually doesn't know how. He protects himself by being critical and superior in social situations, "I don't need these people". He chooses women who will tolerate his control and allow his drinking and drugs. He gets "needy" in an unattractive, unbalanced way and only when he's in a seriously negative mood. People are turned off by his closed, superior attitude. He started using tools and hypnosis to heal these immature wounds. These wounds are not the highest-functioning part of his personality. He has overcome a lot and now owns a good business. He has felt stuck for a long time without any tools to soothe and heal these wounds. He has felt limited by the wounds from his childhood and the worn out defenses that he coped with during childhood. Buried feelings keep him from enjoying people and life more.

**the child
at my
CORE**

age 4- HAVE TO WIN WOUND

- I have to win at everything
- I feel stupid or lazy unless I win or really shine
- I'm anxious, I never feel ok
- I feel criticized a lot, on edge
- I'm "not good enough"
- I'm angry, guarded, defensive
- I only try things I can win at
- I feel insecure, empty
- I am Mom's "winner" and we go to competitions for me to win and shine
- If I don't win Mom gets mad
- I can't be a disappointment

age 4- LITTLE MISS PERFECT WOUND

- I'm wound up, uptight, anxious
- I stay compulsively busy, "on" stressed and "up"
- I feel responsible, serious, rushed and always behind
- I feel like a martyr
- everything feels hard
- I don't relax or have fun
- I'm not spontaneous or creative
- I can't "play", let go, because I might fail or make a mistake
- I have to try harder, I always feel pressured to be "perfect"

age 3- IGNORED-NEGLECTED WOUND

- I have a "to do" list, stay detached, "in my head"
- I'm wound up, uptight, tense
- I'm compulsively busy, stressed
- I'm responsible, serious, rushed
- angry or depressed, lonely
- I'm codependent with others
- I feel empty, needy, when alone
- I wasn't allowed to be a child
- I was more of a "doll" for Mom

A Pressured-Competitive Woman

This educated, bright professional woman has been troubled by these core wounds that have held her back from being close to people. Because she felt so criticized inside, she wouldn't lean on anyone emotionally, or let others "get in". She picked men who treated her like she treated herself, who ignored her needs and feelings, like she was learned to do. She got "needy" in an unattractive, unbalanced way and only when she was seriously stressed out. She was sick a lot. Mom pressured her from the time she was a baby to win "baby pageants" and to give her lonely mother a social life. She felt tremendous pressure to be a perfect little miss winner, so Mom had goals and dreams. This woman was programmed to be used and exploited by others, to feel needed. She allowed men to criticize and pressure her, just as her narcissistic mother did. These wounds are not the highest-functioning part of her personality which she used to get out of feeling stuck. Her wounds had a great deal of intense anxiety she used medication for. She worried about her own parenting skills. She tends to give her kids pep talks and she isn't fun to be around. Her kids are "very good" all the time, just as she is. The problem is kids aren't supposed to be so serious.

age 4 –MOMMA'S BOY WOUND
- Mom needed me to listen and take care of her, I was special
- Mom demanded all my time, we were "best friends"
- When she calls, I feel guilty and anxious and can't say no
- I feel empty, needy, anxious or moody, depressed when alone
- I can't relax or have fun
- I'm not spontaneous or free
- I can't "play", let go, feel ok
- I'm careful, guarded, tense
- I married a woman who is too needy and she's a turn off

age 5-WOUND UP TIGHT WOUND
- I've always felt insecure
- I'm guarded, defensive
- I don't try many things
- I feel empty when I slow down and I get antsy inside
- I can't sleep, I stay up late
- I have to have everything "just right", in its place
- I'm a perfectionist
- my life is like a small safe box with my routines
- I feel anxious at work so I work at home
- I have road rage

the child at my CORE

age 6 – LONER WOUND
- I'm self-conscious socially
- I watch myself, censor myself
- I feel judged, uncomfortable
- I feel drained socially
- I'm distant with others
- I am alone most of the time
- I only feel ok when I'm by myself, I'm used to it
- I withdraw and hide out
- I'm only safe with Mom
- I didn't play with other kids or join clubs or groups
- People don't interest me

A Man Who Doesn't Like Sex

This man's core wounds have caused him to create an insulated lifestyle that lacks fun, change or growth. He is bored and unstimulated by any real dreams or goals. He married a woman like his mother who is needy and dependent. He never resolved his anger so it builds up into road rage and he explodes or gets depressed in predictable moods. He basically feels trapped by his wounds. They have held him back from being close to people, from making friends, from feeling nourished in healthy ways. He's too uptight to enjoy much. He doesn't let anyone get too close or really "get in", wasn't close to anyone growing up and isn't used to closeness. He isolates himself in a safe, small world and tells himself "I don't need people". People are turned off by his closed, uptight, serious superior attitude. He started using tools and hypnosis to heal these immature wounds. These wounds are not the highest-functioning part of his personality. He turned off to his wife because of his anger at being so enmeshed with his mother most of his life. His anger was projected onto his wife and he shut her out. Because core wounds are always immature (formed when we are children) his wounds made his wife a replacement for Momma. He resented her neediness but it was familiar. He felt controlled by her neediness and her dependency. This also kept him from having to see himself as he really is which is also dependent and needy. He was withholding of sex to punish his controlling wife-mother. He is too passive and immature to feel like a man with her. It's a vicious cycle.

Identifying my own 2-3 Core Wounds

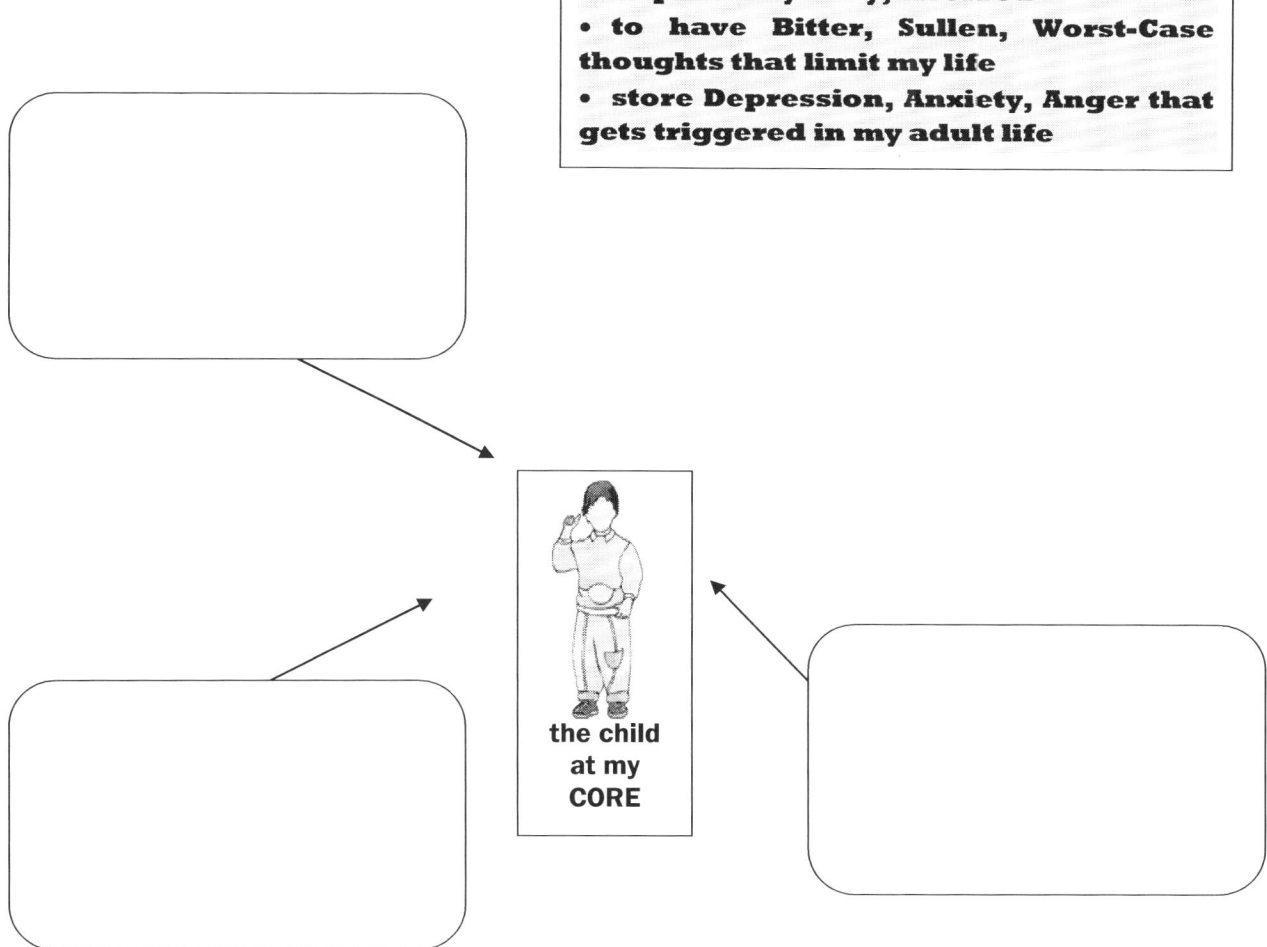

Core Wounds Get Triggered
- to have Negative Moods that persist and recycle, can be a burden
- to Overreact to everyday slights
- to Limit My Lifestyle and avoid new experiences, keeps me in a "box"
- to feel Wound Up Inside or too dependent on Addictions, or being Compulsively busy, stressed
- to have Bitter, Sullen, Worst-Case thoughts that limit my life
- store Depression, Anxiety, Anger that gets triggered in my adult life

the child at my CORE

Identifying my own 2-3 Core Wounds

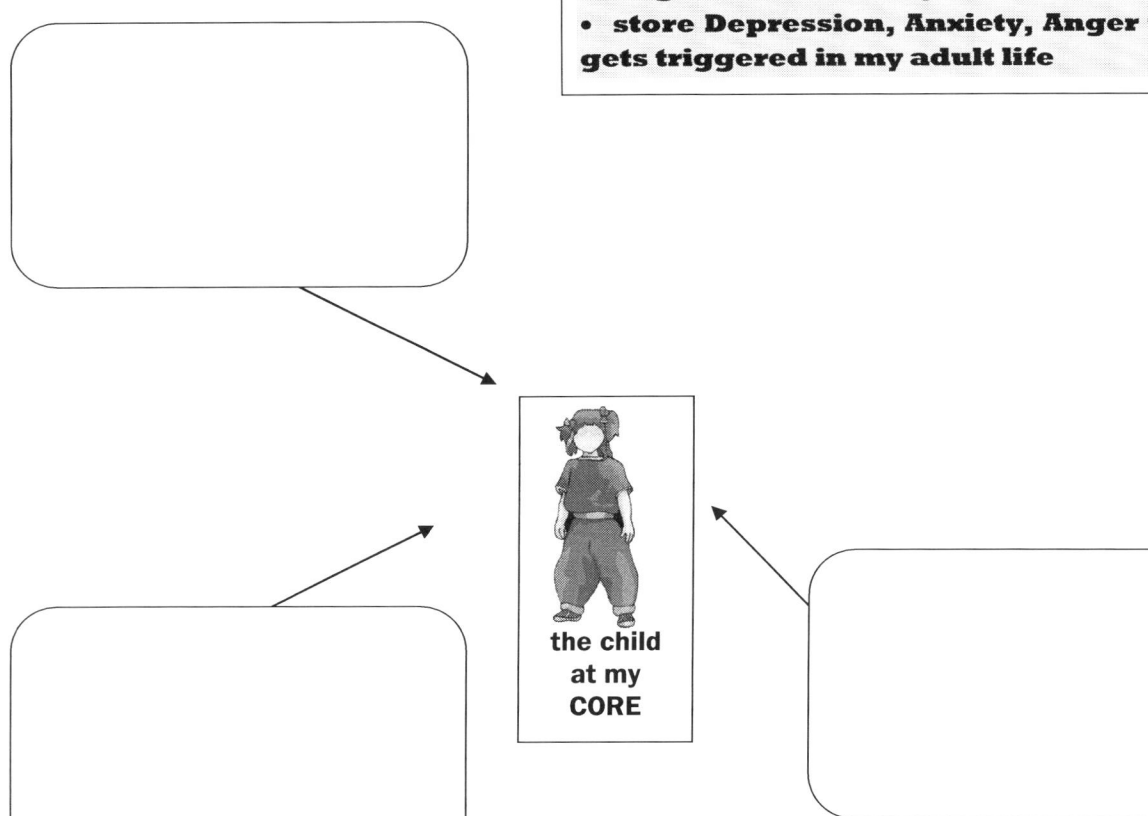

Core Wounds Get Triggered
- to have Negative Moods that persist and recycle, can be a burden
- to Overreact to everyday slights
- to Limit My Lifestyle and avoid new experiences, keeps me in a "box"
- to feel Wound Up Inside or too dependent on Addictions, or being Compulsively busy, stressed
- to have Bitter, Sullen, Worst-Case thoughts that limit my life
- store Depression, Anxiety, Anger that gets triggered in my adult life

the child at my CORE

the child
at my
CORE

USING THE CHILD AS A TOOL

*healing my core wounds, feelings
*changing my moods and triggers
*getting "out of my head", detached
*supporting, healing negative moods
*being healthier in my dependency
*creating a healthier, open lifestyle

the child
at my
CORE

UNDERSTANDING MY "CHILD" TOOL

- the child is narcissistic by nature "me, me, me"-it is self-absorbed which is natural for its survival and development; this isn't healthy in adults, it's normal in "the child"

- the child lacks impulse control-so it is demanding, impulsive and wants it right now, but is also resilient and its natural impulsive needs can be met many ways

- the child can't delay gratification-it wants its needs met right this minute, but using the adult tools gives your child the attention, support it often needs to feel full

- in adults the child is the immature part of the personality-it can't see the big picture, it is "childish", it lacks maturity, this part of the personality isn't a mature part

- the child is fun, it plays, it laughs out loud, it is the de-stressor in our life, it is creative, spontaneous, and it needs "time out" for fun; it makes life exciting

- the child is a raw emotional reaction-it's feelings are often intense and overreactions; it's important to know its feelings because it is a great sensor/reactor

- the child is moody- it's storage for core wounds and buried feelings that can cause triggered moods in adults; these core wounds can be healed using tools

- the child stores patterns internalized from childhood-patterns inherited from our parents become how we relate and react in a relationship; it's not usually healthy

- the child wants to be taken care of by someone external (or a drug, a pill, an addiction), a "fix"- the child demands and expects this unless tools are used

- the child has cravings, emotional habits, addictions that it can't change without support- using tools gives the child a way to manage its wound up feelings

- the child lacks empathy, can't take responsibility, is too immature to have a higher level relationship-the adult part of the personality can connect in healthier patterns

- the child is defended with worn out defenses that limit life for adults-it's controlling, closed, blaming, has triggers, wounds, is too needy and unhealthy in its dependency

- the child at the core needs to be nourished, guided, made to feel safe and accepted with enough internal support to enjoy life, the adult tool can give this to the child

THIS IS ALL "NORMAL" FOR CHILDREN
AND THEY ARE SUPPOSED TO BE THIS WAY!

Don't Be an Emotional Burden!
Core wounds cause Relationship Problems

When you're gonna blow, take a break!

Your intimate relationship is fragile. Venting intense anger causes a vicious cycle, even if it's the silent kind. Cool down, then approach your partner with what you need, feel, want to discuss. Intense anger is not appropriate in healthy relationships. If anger escalates too quickly and you find you are often triggered with so much anger you can't have reasonable conversations, you may have a core wound that is surfacing and getting in the way of communication.

Your partner isn't really doing this to you!

No he/she isn't, no matter how you feel! This is a childhood pattern from families with poor communication. This is caused by unhealthy dependency not your partner! You can begin to express feelings, needs, and open up and ask for healthy communication from your partner. You may want to learn some communication skills and how to set some healthy, mature boundaries. This is not the way to approach a relationship and it's usually a result of a core wound.

You need a new lifestyle! This isn't healthy!

If your lifestyle isn't healthy, has too much stress, has addictions or problems with compulsive issues, work with your partner to make some changes. If you have addictions or compulsive issues (staying too busy) you need to work on your core wounds and buried feelings. A healthy relationship needs you to bring some real energy to it, to "be there" with the highest-functioning part of yourself, not the most wounded part! Acting out core wounds causes unhealthy lifestyles.

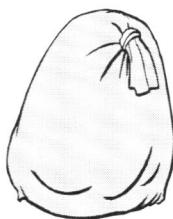

Are you carrying around a lot of old baggage?

We have all lived a long time and have a lot of reasons to stay full of resentments, to be bitter, to say "I knew it". Being intimate means growing out of old baggage and letting go of the past. Being "right" can be very lonely. Holding onto grudges keeps the "wall" between you and your partner. Buried anger and pain needs to be healed! Core wounds are usually what causes these feelings to get triggered as negative beliefs, unhealthy attitudes, sour moods. Use tools to let it go!

GROWING OUR RELATIONSHIP TOGETHER

HEART-CENTERED LOVE

PROGRAMMING
stuck in unhealthy
patterns

REPROGRAMMING
a higher level of
love

Growing Together-
A more Heart-Centered Love

Week 8	Reprogramming Tools Exercises, Homework and Tools
Growing Together- A more heart-centered love	• Tools not Talk! • The Lowest Level of Love • How Couples use Tools • We aren't entitled to Heart-Centered Love

TOOLS not TALK!

Couples want to move to a **higher level of love**, with mature boundaries, healthier dependency, communication where they "feel heard", and to be more nourished as a couple. Talking about it is like talking about weight loss, it's a great idea but doesn't make much happen. Just processing your current fight, even gaining great tidbits of analytical insight, isn't enough to make substantial changes in patterns. You need to become **actively involved in your growth process** in order for changes to stick! Old patterns are simply too natural and automatic and they insidiously creep back in. Tools make each partner responsible for bringing higher-functioning behavior into the relationship.

Tools provide couples with a way to "get out of their head", be less general, global and analytical and begin to connect in a more authentic fashion. Too often couples confuse emoting and erupting in a flurry of angst and emotional drama with real connection. Emoting and erupting in emotional drama is **not the stuff of healthy connection and communication**. Any 14 year old can do this. Acting out a lot of negative moods is so needy! When this is going on it's usually a lot of blaming, venting, or being adversarial in some fashion. In a lot of cases when we're upset we're too reactive, enmeshed and immature at that moment and aren't taking our 50% of the responsibility for healthier boundaries. Of course we usually blame our partner for this! Tools help you maneuver through this tangled mess of hurt, anger and confusion and need.

The Wounded Child has New Shoes

The ever-familiar wounded child now has new shoes to wear. This popular tool has been used for years for individual and personal growth. Now we can use it for couples work too! The wounded child is a tool to help couples take some new steps in growing their relationship. Couples use tools to identify their patterns so they can replace them with better choices, that feel more nourishing. We need to use tools to do this or it stays too vague. Tools are based on some "hypothetical constructs" that are ideal for couples to access their highest-functioning, most mature behavior and attitudes and then use it internally to dialogue with their most wounded, immature, unhealthy reactions. **A process called shifting** takes advantage of what we already do naturally. We talk to ourselves in our head all day long anyway... so we might as well put this normal everyday tendency to work for us! We can use two dynamic hypothetical constructs called **the adult**, to access healthy, mature patterns, and **the wounded child,** to locate the stuff that keeps love stuck. This gives us some control to be able to change behavior and improve relationships. It's actually a lot easier than it sounds.

To begin to increase your awareness of your child self, simply let the child talk, vent, react, and have all of its learned attitudes, old feelings, pent up reactions, and immature needs. Remember the child was formed, conditioned and wounded during childhood. The wounded child is programmed with patterns, moods, reactions from your past. Although it's interesting to know where they came from, it's even more important to have a tool to stop relating this way. It makes sense for it to be somewhat immature and in most of us, it's not healthy. Our goal is not to change the child so much as it is to become aware of how it's wounded, the patterns it's reacting to our partner with, and to help the child feel better. The child part of the personality is fragile and vulnerable and needs the mature, healthy guidance and support of the inner adult. When we consistently react to our partner with the most wounded part of our personality, it causes resentment. No one wants to take care of another adult's wounds. We're each responsible for our own wounds, negative moods and triggers. Acting them out is just giving your child free reign with no internal support. It's emotionally irresponsible and immature and causes the lowest level of love. Your partner will push you away eventually if this is how you express needs and feelings. Emotional trust will be low and your partner will turn off to you, losing attraction and desire. Your child is not programmed or capable of a higher level of love. This is ok because you have another part of your personality to use that can make love more wonderful.

Use your Adult for Nourishing Love

When you learn to **shift out of the unhealthy, immature patterns** in your child, you're more able to open up your relationship, to feel more nourishing to your partner, to communicate in patterns that don't escalate. By locating them in the wounded child part of your personality you're able to **shift out of these patterns.** The adult part of your personality is **the tool to access higher-functioning, healthier, more mature behavior.** You may decide to work with a couples therapist for a few months to **reprogram your adult** with healthier, new patterns that make love feel nourishing. The adult is a great tool. You can reprogram it to heal core wounds, to release buried feelings that keep getting triggered, to work with your addictive or compulsive wounded child issues, to communicate in more inviting ways that bridge the gap with your partner. Acting out the patterns your wounded child is programmed with is what causes the epidemic number of divorces we're struggling with today. At best it causes relationships to feel distant and troubled with unhealthy dependency issues instead of nourishing love. The table on the next page shows the programmed patterns that keep love from being the rich, full heart-connected vision of love we want it to be. As couples use tools they can shift out of the programming in the child, and begin to be the nourishing partners that makes love have depth and substance.

This isn't working!
The lowest level of love isn't nourishing!

We are Enmeshed, don't have Healthy Boundaries	• Codependent patterns: tries to please, "buy", or is a rescuer, caretaker, tolerates an immature partner • Partners don't have healthy emotional boundaries together, don't expect enough mature behavior • One partner leans on the relationship in unhealthy dependency patterns: can feel like a burden
Our Communication Ends, Stays Superficial "on the surface", or it Escalates	• Resentments builds walls between us and we are: "roommates" or "act out" anger frequently • We can't "talk" and feel heard, get problems resolved • We aren't a team, have power-struggles, feel like we are adversaries working against each other • We tend to have denial, avoidance, minimizing issues • One of us may argue, nag, have heavy "talks", vent, pout or "become edgy" to get attention for moods
We aren't Emotionally Connected Enough- We live "in our head"	• A partner is stuck "blaming", not being open enough • A partner doesn't take their own responsibility for problems, won't "own" their 50% of why it's an issue • A partner is detached, lives "in his/her head" • Compulsive issues cause love to stay "on the surface" • We stay fine, busy, disconnected, or detached and don't know feelings, needs in a flowing way • We overreact when we get triggered or when we get moody, pick fights, feel entitled to act it out
Our Emotional Trust is too Low	• Partners act out negative moods, triggered feelings • We don't approach each other from the highest-functioning parts of ourselves that invites intimacy • Emotional trust is low and our relationship isn't nurturing, warm, supportive enough emotionally • We aren't "there for each other" emotionally
We don't Nourish each other in Mature, Reciprocal ways	• Partners aren't nourished in reciprocal, balanced ways, it's one-sided because one partner is needy • One partner is passive-aggressive or self-absorbed and wants to stay in a childish position with the other • Desire problems, sexual demands, needy sex used as a "fix" or a substitute for mature, healthy closeness

Using Tools
couples who use tools to change patterns

> **He's turned off and she nags.**
> Mike is surly and stays in his own world, a couch potato, who shuts her out. Mary nags because he isn't fun, is irritable when they finally go out, and he rarely initiates sex. She lectures but feels powerless. She has two positions: to threaten divorce when she blows up or to tolerate his distance. She feels "innocent" and blames it all on him.

Mike and Mary have no insight into what causes their distance. They are both unhealthy in their dependency and the relationship is a crutch for their unhealthy lifestyles. Mary has no personal goals and is somewhat smothering with their daughter, who is in fourth grade. Mary uses her daughter as an excuse to justify staying home, yet she doesn't want to cook meals, cleans only sporadically, and does few of the jobs a stay-at-home Mom usually does. Mike complains because he has to cook his own meals, do his laundry himself, and he feels cheated. She is bossy, controlling, and argumentative. They have money problems but she doesn't want to work even part time. Mike is emasculated and feels controlled. Mary is powerless but dominating. No wonder they have no spark in their sex life. She is having migraines but she denies how unhappy she really is. Mike is feeling depressed and started having a few extra beers lately.

[Mike needs to use his adult to get a voice about his resentments but he is afraid Mary will get a divorce if he doesn't let her have her way. He is dependent on her for their social life. He has no interests or friends. She arranges their social events (and everything else). He can't set reasonable boundaries because he is too unhealthy in his isolation and dependency. Tools for Mike need to address taking some steps to make a few friends, do some things independent of her, build some interests. The relationship shouldn't be a small box he hides out in. His life has become boring to him and it feels empty of fun or nourishment. He has a core wound of being a "loner" that he started to use tools with.

Mary is also frustrated and needs to see how controlling and emasculating her way of talking to Mike is. She has to review her role at home and gain empathy for Mike. Her unhealthy dependency is keeping her "going through the motions" with no personal dreams to fulfill her. Her prior job wasn't satisfying so she doesn't want to work. She is somewhat rigid and negative about trying to make changes. She is fairly invested in being controlling and righteous and needs to use the adult tool to start to take some responsibility for their marriage. Blaming it on Mike keeps them both stuck and angry.]

*They each took steps to build the adult and learn how to take more responsibility for making changes. Here are some of the steps they worked on in couples therapy.

Step 1. Their relationship was closed when they started therapy. They stayed on the surface unless they fought and blew up at each other. They had almost no insight into their causes and were stuck in blaming each other, focused on the symptoms. They initially had to open up their relationship and listen to each other. They were both defensive so this wasn't easy. This increased their insight into the causes of their resentment and distance. Nothing could change until they identified some of their patterns. Mike is passive-aggressive and shut down, silently punishing her for not taking care of him. Mary is more outwardly complaining but doesn't take any responsibility for being a reciprocal nourishing partner. They both have unhealthy lifestyles that are too dependent and use the relationship as both a crutch and a hide out. She talks to him as if he's a child, partly because he acts like it with her. He is adolescent in his lifestyle, being a couch potato to a controlling Mom he shuts out and gives nothing to. They began to listen with more of an open heart to how each of them is feeling deprived and distant.

Step 2. They needed to move out of blaming and become a team. This "roommates" couple was distant and angry underneath a surface of denial and avoidance. Using the adult-child tools they each learned to allow the child to vent and blame in order to listen to their real feelings. The adult was used to move out of blaming and to stop being adversarial, punishing each other silently.

Step 3. The adult is the tool that is capable of taking 50% of the responsibility and expressing needs and feelings in a more open, inviting, mature way. Mary grew into her adult when she was able to recognize her 50%, increase her empathy for Mike, and use her adult voice to expect more mature behavior from him, as he did from her.

*partial sample journaling from Mary as she grew into taking some responsibility for issues, for her anger, for the distance.

Mary's child: Why doesn't he ever act fun? He's so mean and grumpy. He doesn't want sex with me anymore. Other men flirt with me! Why do I have to put up with his moods. What's he doing for me? Why should I even stay married! (The child blames, complains, vents, etc. but it is important to hear the child's needs and feelings.)

Mary's adult: Child, you are being so one-way again. You're blaming everything on Mike. We have learned we aren't the "innocent victim". Mike has his point of view too. He's mad because we're being selfish. I didn't see that before but I do now. Mom is bossy and controlling and Dad just took care of himself, he allowed it, so I guess I came by it honestly. But I don't want their marriage…yuk! I need to take some responsibility for my own life too. I'm in a rut and so is Mike. Our world has become so routine and boring. We haven't had a date in a long time. No wonder we don't have sex. We don't have any heat, any fun or romance, and we're never alone anyway. I stay busy with Betsy and he watches TV. I won't go to work this month, but I am glad we're facing this, even if I do have to start cooking! I haven't wanted to take care of Mike because he doesn't nurture me. I can meet Mike in the middle and be a more nourishing partner. I'm going to expect him to be more of an adult partner to me too. He really is adolescent and I want a man!

Mary's child: So fine, now I cook and clean and I still feel deprived. I'm just as mad!

Mary's adult: Doing our part of being a stay-at-home Mom is just one step. I won't leave it at that! He feels I am a spoiled child and am not listening to his needs. Child as much as I hate to admit it, we know it's true. I do feel entitled to have him pamper me. I want him to "man up" so I guess I need to be a grown up too. I will talk to him about bringing more energy to our dates and taking some initiative to be more of a lover to me. I'm not going to nag. I'm going to use my adult voice. That way he does listen and take me seriously. All this time I thought my anger was my power and now I see how it made him tune me out. I would tune that out too! I can't blame him.

This couple did weekly homework 10 minutes a day only 3X a week to gradually **build the adult** in each of their personalities. They used an email program with their therapy, between sessions, which helped them become more connected and also allows the therapist to see what they needed to work on. Building the adult takes practice and repetition but it has the added benefit of making each of them feel heard. They didn't initially know how to talk openly, take responsibility for making changes, or move out of blaming and punishing each other. They used the **adult voice** as a tool to stop escalating, changing the subject and becoming defensive.

They both wanted their marriage to grow but **the child part** of each of them had been building a case and feeling deprived for a long time. This kept them stuck with a wall and almost no affection, fun, nourishment. They had to open their hearts again. On the surface they thought they were loving but they were stuck being very angry and controlling. Mary didn't know how to nourish her husband emotionally and she had to grow in this area. She had thought she was totally open with all of her complaints and venting. In fact she was as closed and shut down as he was. Venting and blaming isn't being open. If it was no one would feel distant! Her migraines actually improved as she opened up to herself and learned to be less angry and manage some of her moods with tools. She also learned how to set mature boundaries so she felt taken seriously and wasn't so frustrated.

The **workbooks have part one and part two** so they aren't cumbersome to use. Part two has to do with building the adult in more detail, learning to expect more of a heart-centered connection, and how to set healthier boundaries. Building the adult to do all this and to be able to use the adult voice for communication promotes a higher level of intimacy.

> **He needs sex every day.**
> Bert is stressed and complains about traffic and how hard he works. He demands sex every day or he gets moody. Diane gives him his "fix" because she feels anxious if he's mad. She doesn't have any desire anymore. She tells herself it's her duty. He criticizes how she performs sexually and how bored he is with her. She tries but fails.

Bert is actually not the "lover" he thinks he is. In fact he uses sex like an addict, to unwind. It's not about connection, sharing, loving or affection. It's about his "fix" that he's owed, because he feels entitled for being so stressed out. Even when they go out together he's preoccupied and talks about himself. He doesn't nourish her and actually isn't able to connect emotionally. He's either complaining about his stresses or talking about his successes. Diane is his audience. Bert has a core wound of needing to be "on", to be the center of attention. Diane has a core wound of being the good, busy child who is compulsively trying to be perfect. They both need to work on those wounded parts of themselves so they can shift into their adults. Diane is not a victim, she is more of a dependent, pleasing child than a mature woman, where he's concerned (like her mother was). She doesn't voice her real feelings or needs because she's too detached and scattered mentally. Staying this disconnected from her buried feelings is causing her so much anxiety she can't sleep. Their angry wall is likely to get thicker over time, unless they open up their relationship. As needy and demanding as Bert is he may eventually cheat on her, since he lacks insight into why they are stuck. They both blame each other. This relationship is unhealthy in almost every dimension. They lack open communication, they aren't friends or a team, they are both shut down emotionally and too disconnected inside to even know what's going on. He's wound up so tight, he will certainly have health problems. Diane has so much anxiety she gives in and takes a pleasing, codependent, submissive role. She silently seethes about how men are and inside builds a case against Bert. She feels tired a lot, has too many aches and pains. They stay on the surface because he runs over her and talks down to her when they do try to talk. She doesn't know how to focus on real issues anyway so communication stays surface.

[This couple is on autopilot, going through the motions, living life like it's a treadmill. They both suffer from the lowest level of love. Love isn't nourishing them. To improve this marriage they each need a few months of using tools on their energy, to become more connected and to build some insight. They both have very little to bring to love. Their lifestyle is too compulsive, they fill time and stay busy and distracted. They aren't connected to how empty they each feel because they ignore their real feelings and stay busier and overextended. Superwoman doesn't need, lean, isn't open! Bert's only way to connect is with addictive, immature sex. He's angry because he feels she tolerates him and he isn't nourished. He feels if he doesn't guilt her (you owe me) and pressure her (I'll get mad) he will get nothing from her, which is true, but he isn't capable of more either. As wound up as he is, he needs a release, a fix, and settles for crumbs. After all he's only giving crumbs. They're stuck and their hearts aren't open to each other.
This is actually a high-functioning professional couple, just unhealthy in love. Bert needs to use some tools to build his adult and actually become aware of how he approaches her and why he turns her off. He isn't a "lover" to her. His adult can take responsibility for changes and learn how to "get out of his head". He used some hypnosis to connect with his core wound inside, his neglected child that feels so deprived and has to grab an audience. Using tools he started to heal this needy part of his child. He began to feel less wound up as well. He actually did more homework than she did because she was resigned and felt nothing would work. She was dependent and shut down and wanted him to change first. She stayed in a blaming pattern for quite a while. I told him to work on building his adult and to begin to grow and bring that more masculine, nurturing part of himself into their sex life. Months later she began to pick up some slack and move out of her "righteous, innocent victim" child position. She recognized she was also having angry sex, not just him. When they started to work together they really moved forward.]
*They each took steps to build the adult and learn how to take more responsibility for making changes. Here are some of the steps they worked on in couples therapy.

Step 1.: One of their first steps was to "get out of their heads", reduce some anxiety from being so wound up, and begin to get connected to themselves emotionally. This gradually improved their energy with each other, and even more importantly with themselves. Bert's disconnect kept him immature and needy, often approaching Diane in sullen moods. She felt he was an emotional burden, and he was. What she didn't see is that she was also in a child's pattern of being dismissive, critical and superior with him. They both denied issues at first.

Step 2.: They were angry adversaries inside, who kept the peace by pretending it was "fine". Diane was so angry at being used as a fix, but felt trapped in her dependency and child's patterns of being a pleaser and caretaker. She said she felt smothered by his demands and neediness but blamed it all on him. She needed to identify her own enmeshed, reactive, dependent patterns. Superwoman was shocked to hear this was also unhealthy dependency and to realize she kept their marriage as stuck as he did. There are no victims in love. The wounded child inside is the real victim and over time Diane began to use her adult to shift out of being so stuck in her child.

Step 3.: Building the adult and using the adult voice. The adult is the part of the personality capable of higher-functioning behavior, once it's reprogrammed to shift out of the child's patterns. They each used the adult to open up about how they didn't feel like a team, didn't feel heard, and neither of them really felt nourished by mechanical sex.

*partial sample journaling from Bert as he grew into taking some responsibility for their sex life, for his anger, and for the distance.

Bert's child: All she wants from me is a paycheck. Well she does owe me sex. I didn't get married to do without. It's all I get! I'm due!

Bert's adult: You sound so angry, little guy. Diane does want things on her terms and she is too rigid but I haven't stepped up and talked about anything changing. Of course we didn't get married to stop having sex. I actually do want to get more nourishment and connection out of sex. Pressuring, demanding, and guilting her into it isn't going to get us much.

Bert's child: That's the only way I get anything. Mom and Dad have never really nourished me. I feel so moody because I'm stressed out and anxious all the time. I'm so wound up. I can't even relax. I need a fix!

Bert's adult: Being this wound up is keeping us from making a close connection, much less from feeling calm in our own skin. Let's take care of this empty, anxious mood with the hypnosis CD and you can vent a little and I will listen in our journaling. That way we can feel less hyper. I will start to take care of you and release some of these pent up buried feelings so we can unwind inside. I can feel your anger.

Bert's child: This is a bunch of hooey. I deserve sex. I don't want to take care of myself!

Bert's adult: I am going to take care of this needy, anxious, demanding mood so we don't act it out on Diane. We really are using her in some ways when we deprive her of a real connection and nourishment. I can't let you run the show anymore little guy, you brought us close to divorce. Getting a fix doesn't make it better anyway except for a few minutes. I want to create a real sex life and to have her feel desire and attraction again. This isn't being a mature "lover" little guy. Needy sex is too angry. You feel entitled to it but really it just keeps Diane from feeling close to us. Let's try the CD and hypnosis to connect inside and them journal together. I'm taking control. This is what we're going to do.

This couple used tools to work on building a more nourishing sex life and they began to go on dates that actually felt less like "friends" and more like "lovers".

They worked on being able to connect with core wounds inside that kept them distant and resentful. The added advantage of this was she felt less closed and anxious and he felt less wound up.

Fun, fun, fun.
Jim wants to go off-roading, camping, to get out on the desert and play. He likes Disneyland and takes the kids everywhere. Allie goes along but is bored. This was fun years ago when they were 22. Now they're close to 40 and she wants to have a more adult social life. They have grown apart. Sex is a drag for them. They bicker often.

Jim is still the fun guy Allie married. He hasn't changed, she has. She's become more interested in art, politics, culture. Jim actually admitted all that stuff bored him. She complains he's like a boy in a man's life. Jim is tongue-tied and shy socially, like his Dad was. He hasn't grown and learned to have confidence around people so he shies away. He wants Allie to do his interests and go on the outings he plans, which don't much involve taking her places she would enjoy. His outings involve the kids, are usually adolescent in nature and most of the people they meet are in their early 20's. She feels he has a case of arrested development. She wants to have a more stimulating social life. He says yes but resists. They rarely have fun. Dates are tense. He is shy and expects her to "pull teeth" and has excuses why he doesn't talk to her. He doesn't enjoy dates and isn't a mature companion. She thinks about other men lately.

[This couple got married very young and have grown, as we all do. The problem is they haven't grown together. They have no couples interests that they feed their marriage with. Jim is stuck because he unconsciously wants Allie to mother him too much, "pull teeth" on dates, initiate all their plans, give him sex without expecting a mature, reciprocal connection. He has a right to expect all this because she's always done it. Just recently she is so tuned out he's a little worried. Allie was severely abandoned as a child (foster home) and every time she tries to ask for mature behavior or set any boundaries, he simply pulls away and she panics and "fixes it" by giving him needy sex. She is quite verbal and strong on the outside but her abandoned child's core wound keeps her clingy and desperate. He's upset feeling like roommates and she's bored.]
*They each took steps to build the adult and learn how to take more responsibility for making changes. Here are some of the steps they worked on in couples therapy.

Step 1.: Their first step was to learn how to stop bickering. They were either on the surface or bickering and angry. Communication was completely stuck. They were actually invested in their distance (it was comfortable) as roommates so they picked fights most weekends. This kept them from noticing the distance, boredom and loneliness. They both used homework to begin to journal from their child's feelings, all the resentment and needy feelings inside. Office sessions gradually helped them hear these feelings without being defensive and making excuses. They opened up about how lonely they both were.

Step 2.: Growing as a team. This couple each need tools to heal their core wounds. He needs the adult to support him in some baby steps to have a lifestyle outside the small constricted life his child has withdrawn to. She needs tools to deal with expressing her needs with the adult voice instead of blaming and venting. They both want to improve their sex life. Dates are a touchy and difficult issue for this couple. They have been unsupportive and adversarial about dates.

Step 3.: Growing into more mature dates. Dates won't solve all their problems but it will give them some adult ways to begin to nourish each other. This is actually sophisticated. It isn't as easy as it sounds or they'd have done it long ago. They need to feed their relationship because it's starving! They each have fun "in their own worlds", doing things separately. She does things with her friends. He does things with the kids and has her tag along, but the activities aren't about nourishing her as an adult woman. He doesn't nourish her in this way, even forgets her birthday. They have no fun as a couple. He is complaint and promises to change and do things, but then has excuses for staying stuck. She feels she has to drag him along if they do date.

*partial sample journaling from Allie's journaling as she grew into expecting more mature behavior and having an adult voice

Allie's child: I am so fed up with our dates. He makes me wrong and makes it all my fault if I say anything! He's such a bully. He says he's trying but he isn't. It's the same old. I still have to "pull teeth" and do everything.

Allie's adult: Jim doesn't want real changes, he is going through the motions. He doesn't want to nourish me as a man.

Allie's child: Yeh! He is a bore. Plain and simple. He doesn't flirt with me or even try to bring fun energy. I keep telling him! No wonder I don't like sex. Nothing is ever about me!

Allie's adult: That isn't working for us. He feels more criticized. I feel like a teacher giving him a lesson on how to be on a date. No wonder we're stuck. I will ask him to work on shifting and bringing his adult on dates. I'm going to plan some fun and stimulating dates once a month. I will go on one of his if he'll go on one of mine. Maybe we will find some couples things we both like. He is so narrow and constricted in his interests that I will get a list of 20 some odd things I think would be fun and let him choose a few. We'll talk more about sex in our therapy. How do you feel child about me, the adult, planning some dates?

Allie's child: I'm still mad. I still have to do everything. If I plan the dates I still have to be like his mother.

Allie's adult: We both got married very young and never really dated in these new ways. Since I'm the one who wants it I will take some responsibility for making things happen. Complaining will get us nowhere. I will introduce changes and then talk more openly about expecting him to "man up". I think he will if he gets used to new things and feels some confidence. Child you are so black and white in your thinking. We want to grow out of being "mothering" all the time, we don't have to be so rigid about it. Let's make this fun. It will feel more inviting to Jim and less like a test he's going to fail. I want to open my heart to him more and see how he feels.

Over the next 6 months this couple began to work together on these issues and to grow out of being stuck. They began to have more fun together.

Why do I have to work so hard?

You want a lot more out of your relationship!

We enter relationships because we want romance, nourishment, support, and to be energized from the close, warm passion of a loving relationship. Instead we often end up with mechanical sex, feeling we aren't on the same team, being criticized, taken for granted, drained of energy and have too much emotional distance. We settle for much less than the potential we wanted when we began our relationship full of promise, hoping and dreaming of a deeper love. Intimate relationships hold the potential of a great deal of love and joy. In most cases, your relationship will have some of the patterns you were programmed with in the twenty or so years you were in your family. These are usually only as healthy and intimate as your parents and the level of closeness they had, even with you as their child! This is your automatic, default, and natural way to have a relationship. That's great if you want your own intimate relationship to be as fulfilling as Mom's and Dad's. Most of us want more! When Mom and Dad were young they didn't have the tools for a deeper love with emotional support and the nourishment of being mature, equal partners. Our vision and expectation of love and intimacy has grown up. Today we have the vision of a higher level of love. Now we have the tools, skills, and exercises to make it real. We can reach our potential and raise distant, abusive, or enmeshed relationships to a more heart-centered love.

It's too expensive! It takes too much time! Why do I need to do all this?

We spend money on specialists who have been trained to provide us with the services and products we value and make our priorities. We have personal trainers, hair stylists, auto body repairmen, cardiac specialists, plastic surgeons, wedding planners, coaches, massage therapists, even dog trainers! Historically therapists and marriage counselors have treated mental illness and psychological problems, but that eventually led to the Human Potential Movement! Therapists today are trained to guide couples in growing out of dysfunctional, distant or immature patterns that keep love from being more nourishing. The relative fees for a therapist are actually reasonable especially when compared with other specialists we rely on. A well trained therapist will provide you with tools, exercises, materials and a great deal of time and energy. It's a lot more than the typical "talk" session that you may have been used to! Love really is a good investment and it always appreciates! We build our whole life on love. Isn't it worth it?

No one's entitled to a higher level of love!
Are you willing to grow into a level of love that's more nourishing and satisfying?

STUCK!
At Risk for a Broken Family, a Broken Heart

Be honest with yourself!

- Do you feel nourished, fulfilled, and satisfied with it the way it is now?

- Do you feel stuck, bored, angry and feel you have to just tolerate it the way it is?

- Would you stay in this relationship if you could choose all over again today?

USE TOOLS!
Personal and Relationship Growth

Would you like to see some healthy changes?

- If your partner made some changes would you feel more attracted?

- Would you be willing to do your 50% of the growth to make these changes?

- Does settling for distance, abuse, or unhealthy love feel like the only choice?

A HEALTHIER PARTNER
and a
Higher Level of Love

Would you grow to be able to love at a higher level!

- Would you work with your partner and use tools to open your hearts again?

- Would you like to grow and open up to a higher level of love with more energy?

- Everyone has some "baggage". Is yours keeping your relationship stuck?

WORKBOOK PART 2 will guide you in USING TOOLS to work toward the relationship you've both dreamed of!

See my website for updates on workshops and presentations as well as a list of referrals and resources. I am available to present a workshop in your area. I offer training to therapists interested in using tools and a tool-based homework program. Specific training in using hypnosis with core wounds is also offered.

Special thanks to a special site called **clipart.com** which supplies all of the royalty free art clips that made this material so user-friendly. Clipart images are © 2009 Jupiterimages Corporation

4835551

Made in the USA
Lexington, KY
06 March 2010